REQUIEM

COREY KNEEDLER

Written by Corey Kneedler
Edited by Casey Britain
Cover by Rebecca McCartney

Ghosts of Home

Requiem

© 2021, Corey Kneedler.

ISBN: 978-1-09838-4-791 (print)

Foreword

The subjects in this book may not be suitable for a younger audience. While the terminology is mostly PG-13, there are some difficult and touchy, possibly even triggering subjects mentioned in some of the pieces in this book. While I hope you enjoy this book, please keep that in mind as you read.

"If I leave this life with dreams unrealized, will you continue my legacy? If I should go before the final leaf falls from the trees, will I, in cold winter, be in your memories?" – The Ghosts

Ghosts of Home

These ghosts of home, they call to me. In the twilight hours I can hear them speak.

These ghosts of home, they watch me when I wake and when I sleep.

These ghosts of home, they remind me of a time long passed.

These ghosts of home, they show me that time fades but memories will last.

These ghosts of home, they haunt me every day.

These ghosts of home, they saturate my world in shades of gray.

And if you hear a frightened shrill, look beyond the window sill.

Inside the abandoned house you'll find me, looking for the door that unlocks with this key.

And when I finally find my way out of this place, the sun's warm rays I'll finally embrace.

A new day will rise, and from these cracked walls I will fly.

But for now, these ghosts of home will keep me here.

They will give me comfort in the midst of this crippling fear.

Aquatic Sonnet

Is she drowning or is she dreaming? It's hard to say for certain. What would be seen if she could reveal what's hiding behind that old worn curtain?

It's hard to breathe when oxygen ceases, when her beautiful healthy skin becomes riddled with diseases.

She knows she can't control these waves, but she tries her best to resist them day after day.

How peaceful it must be for her, floating endlessly through the sea.

So euphoric she almost doesn't hear the beeping as her body slowly begins sinking.

Her angelic presence moves like a dancer, drifting here and there, searching for relief with her blank stare.

And on the surface we stand in a circle, holding hands and asking God to take her to the promised land.

As her feet reach the coral reef, for a moment she swears she feels the hope of relief.

Suddenly the seabed below her shakes...

And then the angel wakes.

Bliss

Let's jump into the bottle tonight, baby, as we hold each other tight.

Let the fire inside our hearts burn with delight.

I'll hold onto you with all my might, never let you out of my sight.

Let's take another hit. Let's savor every bit of it.

We'll swim in a sea of hatred and lies that will take the rest of our lives to forget.

Love means everything, baby, so let's take another drink to celebrate.

No fate but what we make, so let's make it a good one while we wait -

Wait for the devil to take us away, to an unholy place that we will embrace.

And our souls will burn with delight, as we fade away into the night.

Let God look down on us with shame as we rip His heart to shreds.

Hope is just a distant memory, and we no longer care.

Give me the bottle; you said we could share!

I'm not trying to start a fight my love, but this isn't fair.

What do you mean I never cared? I gave my darkened soul to you!

"*After you I came to the conclusion that love was just an illusion, just a waste of precious minutes. Now I'm painting a new future for myself, and you're never going to be in it.*" – *The Ghosts*

A Final Fantasy

I'm lying in a hospital bed when she walks into the room.

"Dad? It's me. It's Lilia."

I awake to the sound of her crying.
"Oh, honey, I've been up all night holding her. Can you please take care of this one for me?" My wife asks.
 "Of course," I assure her. I walk into her room, flip on the light and pause for a moment.
"My god, what a beautiful little girl," I whisper, then reach my arms down with a smile and pick her up, holding her until she calms down.
"It's ok, sweetheart. Daddy's here. Everything is going to be ok."

I'm kneeling down on her bedroom floor. She puts a small plastic pink teacup into my hand.
"Hurry, daddy! We're gonna be late for Miss Spearmint's tea party!"

We are lying on the handmade blanket her mother made her on a warm summer evening, looking up at the stars.
"Dad? Do you think UFOs are real?"
"I'm not sure," I replied. "But wouldn't life be a lot cooler if they were?"

My angel stands front and center on the stage, wearing her adorable outfit that her grandma made her. This is her solo. When the melodic words spill from her mouth, I feel so proud.
"You're nailing it, honey," I whisper with a smile on my face that I couldn't hide if I tried.

Graduation day. The ceremony is over. She runs up to me and gives me the biggest, tightest hug I've ever had.

"I did it, dad! It's really over!" She screams with excitement.

"This is all you, honey. You did this! Now it's time to soar to even bigger heights!"

A tangled metallic mass sits before me in a grassy ditch. Fragments of glass crack beneath my feet with each step I take.

She's lying in a hospital bed when I walk into the room.

"Honey? It's me. It's dad."

She's unresponsive. I grab her cold hand and hold it tightly.

Beep...

Beep...

"Honey, we have to go. We're going to be late for Miss Spearmint's tea party!"

Beep...

Beep...

"I think I parked the UFO in the handicap spot. The cops are gonna be onto us any minute, honey. We've gotta split, quick!"

You slowly open your eyes and smile at me. Suddenly the color returns to your face "I'm ready, dad. Let's blow this popsicle stand."

Making sure the coast is clear, I pick you up and carry you outside as quickly as my legs can move. We get to the UFO just in time, right before the cops pull up. I close the hatch and sit you down in the cockpit.

"Punch it, sweetheart! Let's get outta here!"

The UFO hovers upward, stopping for a moment before suddenly blazing into the midnight sky in a flash of light.

Suddenly the main screen turns on and Miss Peppermint greets us. "I've been expecting you two," she announces. "We've saved two very special teacups with your names on them. We will see you soon!"

You look over at me, still in your hospital gown. "Dad, is any of this real? Is...this really happening?"

"Does it really matter, honey?" I ask you. "Let's just enjoy the moment. We've got a whole galaxy of adventures ahead of us."

A long, steady beep fills the room...

"You left me hanging, but while you were gone I decided to do some pull-ups. Now I'm coming back stronger than ever." – The Ghosts

Calendar

Anger comes with summer, forgiveness comes with fall. Sadness comes with winter.

Life rolls downhill and then bounces like a rubber ball.

Tell me, how am I supposed to make sense of it all?

New beginnings come with spring, such beauty in blossoming things.

Fresh air comes with April, life starts over in May.

Crawling through life in June, walking through the desert in July, searching for a better day.

I can't pretend to know how these winding roads will change. With every loss, every gain, every stumble we try so hard to rearrange.

August finds us holding on, wondering where those cooler days had gone.

September comes with a sigh of relief, waiting for the falling of that first dying leaf.

October greets us with messages carried on howling winds, with promises that life could somehow start for us again.

The days pass by like scenery on a train we can't stop. When things go wrong the season crawls, leaving us waiting for that final leaf to fall.

November grows colder as our hearts become older. Voices from the past echo in our minds like the final words of a dead soldier.

"I'm here for you;" "You'll never make it," They tell us, teetering back and forth between encouragement and disdain.

And when the howling wind ceases, we will begin again.

December's snow blankets our world like an empty canvas, providing another chance for mending the broken bridge between us.

With the stroke of a brush, a wave of the hand, we kiss goodbye another year as it fades away into the creator's invisible hands.

When all is said and done, when our souls have swept across this barren land, new hope shines ever so brightly in the distance. We can see it, yet so many of us stop cold in our snowy tracks of resistance.

January, the month of my birth, the first month of a new year, the cradle that brought me to this earth.

The bitter chill threatens death in a cold abyss mired by sharp crystals of despair.

"There's nothing ahead, we are going nowhere."

Although this birth month makes me shiver, surely what's ahead brings far greater things yet to be delivered.

February's path is paved with tiny candy hearts, leading to new romances and hopeless endeavors chased by lonely souls looking for

romantic starts.

Like a chain, these months and the seasons they bring with them bind us together as we continue onward through every kind of weather.

March arrives with one last chill, creating the way for us to once again climb that fateful hill.

Flowers bloom, the bees buzz and the birds once again sing. April returns, bringing with it brand new beauty in all living things.

How much more change can these terrestrial bodies take? How much longer must we wait before we can finally wake?

A calendar is a paper thing, not meant to last, never meant to sing. Yet I observe that numbers and days bring so much happiness and sadness in so many different ways. Are we trapped in the squares of our own destinies? Are our lives boxed in by black lines within this calendar I see hanging in front of me?

Seasons come and go.

Time passes and sometimes slows.

Yet still we grow.

Still, I wonder:

When it's all over, when all is said and done, where will we all go?

Reaching for Respite

In the early morning hours I wake, through the house I tiptoe, not a sound I make.

Past the bedroom where the child lies, sleep little darling, don't make a noise, not even a sigh.

Into the kitchen I flip on the light, searching for respite in the middle of the night.

Into the cabinet my fingers crawl, where are you my honey, my sweet fentanyl?

With the sound of a bottle's rattle, I begin my nonsensical prattle.

"Mommy needs a little pick me up, before I start to throw up."

With shaky hands I open the bottle, grab a tablet as my heart hits full throttle.

Sweat pours from my forehead and saturates my skin. My body quakes while the demon stirs within.

Pour a glass of water - is it just me, or is the room getting hotter?

Down the hatch, relief will soon be here at last.

Fall to the kitchen floor, take a deep breath. How much longer before this causes my death?

Cold floor, restless night. I promise you that one day I'll finally get it right.

"Mommy, what are you doing awake?"

"Honey, I....I just wanted to grab a bite of cake."

"Can...I have some too?"

"...Sure, sweetheart. I'd love to share some cake with you."

Her frown suddenly turns to a smile. She might as well enjoy her daughter's company for a while.

Mother and daughter share a tasty treat so sweet, and hold each other tight in the middle of the night.

Mother realizes in this moment of late night bliss, life won't always be like this. From now on, she'll do everything she can to guard her. From now on, each day she'll try a little bit harder.

And on that night hope returned to her broken heart. Life was reset and she found her new start.

"If I could capture the moon in a jar for you, would you use it as a night light beside your bed? If I write a novel for you, would it ever truly get read?" — The Ghosts

Burgundy

Some look to the heavens for love, some search endlessly for it. When I think of true love found, I look across the room and see her standing there, holding that glass of red wine.

The perfect vision of beauty, her Italian hair illuminated in the sun's rays as she gazes out the window into the city streets below.

That's my angel.

Passionate kisses taste like wine, my lips against her skin on every inch of her heavenly body, gasping for breath as we get lost in an ocean of passion.

To touch the love of one's life is to enter into the gates of paradise, to feel heaven's warmth and taste euphoria in its purest form.

When she gazes into my soul with those beautiful ocean eyes, I want to get lost in her galaxy, swim in her Milky Way, fall into a sea of stars and let gravity pull me inside her.

One more glass of wine. Let's dance in the kitchen with our clothes off, away to the harmony of our infinite love, get lost in each other as time stands still and the world becomes ours.

She is everything, and my heart beats for her eternally.

Every touch, every glance, every deep breath, every sigh, every cry brings us closer to eternity.

In this seventh floor apartment we found truth, passion, trust, ecstasy and love.

I want to forever share these red wine kisses, make her my misses and celebrate everything that this incredible bliss is.

This is us. We are love.

This is love. Eternally.

To your Ghost, My Heart - Filled with Regret

"Nothing you love is lost. Not really. Things, people–they always go away sooner or later. You can't hold them anymore than you can hold moonlight. But if they've touched you, if they're inside you, then they're still yours. The only things you ever really have are the ones you hold inside your heart." -Bruce Coville

Three years old. We're throwing stuffed animals at one another, laughing uncontrollably from a sugar high. We barely know one another, but we're having the time of our lives on grandma's living room floor.

Seven years old. Somewhere in the sunshine-soaked Missouri hills, we're exploring the woods behind your grandma's house. A small army of cats follows behind us, stopping to lick the drops of ice cream we leave behind from our root beer float creamsicles.

Ten years old. Your grandma's funeral at a small cemetery in the Ozarks. I'm sitting there with you on a bench in the cemetery, watching you cry. I don't know how to console you so I give you an awkward hug. I wish we could go somewhere and play hide and seek, but you're not in the mood. I haven't lost a family member before so I don't understand what you're going through.

15 years old. Your grandpa's funeral. When I pull up to the cemetery, I'm overwhelmed with both sadness and excitement. It's been a few years, and we have a lot of catching up to do. I wait till you've finished crying and walk up to you.
"It's good to see you again. How have you been?" I ask you.
"Fine," you tell me. "I'm sorry we haven't had a chance to see one another recently. I've missed you."

Rain begins to pour down on the cemetery.

I've missed you too, but I don't admit it.

I play it cool and pretend like I'm too good to give you the time of day, and walk away from the cemetery without even telling you goodbye.

20 years old. Facebook. We are chatting about the good old days, sharing memories of the adventures we had when we were children.

"You know, you always were my favorite cousin," I told you. "I really wish life gave us more chances to spend time together."

You agreed, and we decided to meet up in town some time to hang out. We make plans and set a date.

21 years old. You drive for three hours from Missouri and arrive at my grandma's house to meet up, but I never show. Grandma calls me on the phone and asks me where I am, but I lie and tell her I'm swamped at work and can't make it. I hang up the phone and my girlfriend in the other room asks me who called. "No one," I tell her. "Just some telemarketer."

26 years old. My grandpa's funeral. When I walk into the church and see you standing there, I'm stunned. You've grown up into such a beautiful woman. You seem so happy. It's good to see you again, even if it is at another funeral.

"You know, we really need to start meeting under better circumstances," I tell you jokingly.

"I know, this is totally crazy, right?" We really need to get together and do something soon," you reply.

This time I agree, and I mean it. This time we will do something together, rekindle that old spark of friendship we had so long ago.

Time passes and our plans fall through once again. Relationships, losses, and life events happen and we get caught up in our own goals and dreams. I make one more effort to talk to you on Twitter, but we don't speak much. You seem to be doing well, though.

30 years old. A cold October day.

Your lifeless body hangs from the ceiling of your apartment. When I heard the news, I nearly collapsed to the floor.

Suddenly life doesn't make sense anymore. My heart fills up with anger and confusion. Questions run through my mind, trying to figure out what happened. What went wrong?

Dark clouds filled with regret pour down on me and I hate myself for not reaching out to you, for blowing you off, words unspoken that I should have said. Could I have in some way helped prevent this?

I don't know. And the answers never come. I pray to God and ask Him for some clarity, but my hardened heart refuses to open up to an answer.

31 years old. Every now and then I think about you, and my heart still sinks down into my chest when I remember what happened. Regret still haunts me, and I can't shake the thought of my selfishness, the cold heart I closed up to you when you wanted to see me.

It should have been me.

The lives you touched while you walked the earth, the positivity you brought to everyone around you, fighting hard for what you believed in. I could never be a fraction of who you were.

But I promise I'll try my best. For you.

Never in my wildest dreams would I have thought to stop and consider the fact that life is actually finite, and that one day it would be too late to say goodbye to you.

It's been a hard lesson to learn, and I can't tell you how sorry I truly am, but I pray that wherever you are, wherever your ghost burns brightly, that you are at peace.

And one day we will meet again somewhere up there, where new adventures will await us. And this time, I'll be there. You can count on me.

"You were the one I'd always hoped for. Now you're just a ghost burning outside my front door." – The Ghosts

Werewolf

They pushed you too far, and now they're going to pay. You've suffered enough, it's time to take their pathetic lives away.

You can feel that tingling going up your spine, your fangs growing sharper and your eyes turning red like wine.

The whiskers grow and a growl echoes from deep within your throat.

Your anger fuels you, you've bottled it up inside. When you're done with them, there will be nowhere left to hide.

Your claws extend sharply outward as you scrape them against the concrete. Now it's time to show them who's the real coward, time to shred them into meat.

Tonight you'll go hunting, tonight they'll be your prey. Tonight they will taste fear, and blood will be sprayed.

The rage inside you burns like it's never burned before, and you'll hunt them down one by one, their ears left ringing from your blood-thirsty roar.

You'll rip their frail bodies limb from limb, and delight as the life is sucked from each and every one of them.

The walls will be painted with crimson fear. Every inch of their bodies ripped from ear to ear.

You can taste it on your tongue, this bloody full moon has only begun.

It's time to wreak havoc upon them, time to expose their every sin.

Inside the church they pray, unaware that soon they'll be your delicious prey.

No one will save them, their time will soon be up. They'll drink their wine one last time from the communion cup.

You are divine vengeance, the punishment they deserved so long ago. Make them suffer, leave some half alive so death will come slow.

Tonight the preacher will pay for what he did to you behind the pulpit when you were only three.

Tonight the horrible deeds he performed will be exposed for all the world to see.

Make him suffer, make him pay, and you'll finally have your sweet revenge on this day.

Show the world that inside this church there is no love. Show the world that they no longer give a fuck.

Your back is hunched up, your fur so thick and coarse, it's time to burst through the doors and go at them full force.

And on that night vengeance was wrought. Blood was spilled as the congregation fought.

But they couldn't stop the werewolf's rage, didn't stand a chance once he'd engaged.

And a corrupt pastor on that fateful day was finally shown the error of his ways.

When the police found him, he was nothing more than a pile of meat. Vengeance, it would seem, was now complete.

A lesson was learned on that bloody night, that what goes on behind sacred closed doors should never be hidden from sight.

And the werewolf howled with vengeful delight.

To a Friend

We're in two different worlds, you and I.

And yet, so long ago we shared the same universe. It seems like a dream, a life that never existed.

The older I get, the more distant those happy memories seem.

I swear that I could see it clearly when I woke up last night. I could see you and me playing outside, basking in the warm rays of sunshine.

For a moment I smiled, recalling how joyous it felt to hold your hand as we frolicked among the clovers, playing hide and seek in the backyard, swinging as high as we could on the swing set.

Funny how you're probably getting high right now, higher than we ever could on those warm summer days.

And yet here I sit, alone in an empty room, sober as can be, with no escape to take me back.

You're probably passed out somewhere, drooling all over yourself. Sounds like a horrible way to end the night. But is it?

I chose the straight and narrow path. I chose sobriety, but was it worth it? Sometimes I wonder who's better off.

When life hits you hard and you've got nothing to numb the pain, what do you do? You sink down into your own mind, swimming in an ocean of madness, your own private hell.

Some days I wish I could be just like you: blissfully unaware of the troubles that surround me. But what price would I pay? If one of us can't keep it together, we're both doomed, aren't we?

No matter how hard you try though, the pain can never truly be erased. You can numb it, but like a cancer it keeps growing and spreading, eventually choking the life out of you.

Who do you suppose is the stronger of us? Your frail body's high tolerance to drugs and alcohol, or my heart and mind being numbed from all the emotional pain I've endured over the years?

I worry about you sometimes. I worry I'll get that text or phone call someday telling me you never woke up. And for some reason I'd blame myself for it. Because I walked away from you so many years ago. When you chose your lifestyle, I didn't agree with it, and I made it very clear. I told you that you were wrong for making that decision. I cursed at you and broke that bracelet you made me. You were in tears and I just walked away, like I didn't give a shit.

Did you know I cried that night?

It's true.

I buried my face in my pillow for four solid nights. I felt so helpless, so angry. I knew I couldn't change your mind no matter what I said.

So I let you go.

Now you're probably lying half naked on a cold floor, halfway across the world. Maybe someone is lying there with you. Maybe you're all alone.

I imagine that high felt pretty good, if only for a single short moment. For a split second you forgot about how miserable you are. And before you had a moment to cry, you probably blacked out, saving yourself the pain.

Some friend I was.

I knew better. Deep inside I knew I should have called you or knocked on your door, anything to try and convince you not to go.

But the one thing I never did that I've regretted all these years is apologize to you.

So I guess that's what I'm trying to do here.

If you ever read this, I'm sorry.

I'm sorry I let you down. I'm sorry I threw away our friendship, and for what it's worth, I'm fucking miserable too.

Funny how we took two separate paths and ended up in the same place, huh?

Life is funny like that sometimes, isn't it?

I hope some day you wake up and read this. I hope someday you know that I never truly went away. The biggest part of me has been there with you the whole time. And I'm still here if you ever want to talk.

And if we never meet again in this life, I'll hang on to the sun-soaked memories we once shared so many summers ago, before the sting of life stabbed us in our hearts.

I pray that you'll remember those days too.

Better to share a moment with someone than to go a whole lifetime without another's company.

I'll see you on the other side, my friend.

"There is such power in words, but your ability to destroy them terrifies me most." – The Ghosts

Questions

Is there more to life than what I'm seeing?

So much more to feel beyond this numb state of being?

As a child I ignored the changing of seasons, but now the passing of warmth into winter forces me to consider all the reasons.

I never much liked being cold, but they say wisdom comes with walking through life's snow and growing old.

How long must I freeze before chilly temperatures kill this disease?

I wonder how many flakes of snow will pass me by as I ponder the reasons why I could never quite fly.

When the ice melts, will I finally find what I've been looking for?

Or will the answers I seek lie behind another season's door?

The Cemetery

How long after we die will loved ones forget to say goodbye? How many decades will pass before our names are buried under the tall grass?

Once flesh and bone, one day gray headstones will become the only way we'll be known.

It's so quiet in this peaceful cemetery. Sometimes it's hard to imagine this is a place where dead bodies are buried.

What ever happened to Madeline and her husband John? Once dancing in fields coated with moonlight, now long gone.

Where did little James run off to? Buried in his grave at age six, 1822.

Henry kissed his wife goodnight on that sad evening before she felt Spanish Flu's final sting, aged nineteen.

Underneath an unmarked grave in the corner of the yard, the bones of black slave Bernard, who gave his life to save his master's daughter, rest forgotten like a faded old postcard.

Such importance these lives once had. Once so young and vibrant with dreams as rich as yours and mine, the thought of their demise makes my heart feel so sad.

How could I ever boast of gifts, power or wisdom in this life, when my life could be cut short suddenly by a sharp knife? Why should I be cocky about anything if one day my bones will rot six feet under in a place where human eyes can no longer see?

Some say the ghosts of yesterday still walk this hallowed ground. I've searched here and there, high and low, but still no spirits have I found.

Perhaps they're quietly resting after living lives full of such sickness and hardship. Or perhaps they've moved on and taken a journey far away from here on an ethereal trip.

Wherever they've gone, I know my time to join them won't be long.

I may have miles ahead of me, or perhaps mere inches. Maybe I'll take my final breath trapped in world war trenches, or perhaps I'll grow old and sit with young lovers holding hands on park benches.

Whatever the case may be, I know there's a few feet of earth somewhere below waiting for me.

I'd better make the most of these moments now, lest generations pass and forget about me somehow.

"If love is your religion, consider me an atheist." – The Ghosts

Narcissist

Her beautiful, candy-coated presence shines brightly when she walks into the room. The room erupts with applause. Cherry red lipstick covers her soft lips, eyes sparkling with illuminating gaze as she flashes a pearly white smile to the crowd.

But underneath it all lies the filth, the poisoned blood, the addiction to passionless love affairs. Her darkened heart beats lifelessly inside a cold, empty soul corrupted by the evils of a cold world.

Inside her brain a demon scratches the walls of her sanity, terrifying screams ringing loudly over the sound of her dying conscience.

She approaches the podium and waits for the applause to die before taking a deep breath.

The words she speaks taste like honey but poison the mind like bitter arsenic:

"I am the victim. I am the scorned. I am not the one to blame. I am flawless. I am everything. I deserve your hearts and I deserve your pleasure. I will take from you and give nothing in return. I've done nothing wrong. I am your queen and I deserve your attention. You will bow before me as I stab you in the back. You will kiss my feet as I cut your heads off with my sword. You will live for me and die for me. I will cut you down and leave not a trace of your dignity behind. I will rip your hearts to shreds and curse you with the very lips I kiss you with. I am perfect. I am the victim."

The crowd of men erupts with a resounding applause as she stands before them with an innocent gaze and a sinister smile.

Sweet as honey, but deadly as poison.

One by one they would find out that the pleasure she brought only led to pain. And she'd devour them until she'd had her fill.

The innocent, flawless victim in a battlefield of broken hearts.

Ornament

Hold steady this old silver ornament as you place it upon the glistening branches of this illuminated tree.

Wipe away the tears and try to replace this empty feeling with the long-lost holiday glee.

Like a mirror, this ornament reflects the memories into your mind's eye - takes you back to the days before you were just trying to survive.

Who is that staring back at you from inside this mirrored globe? Look closer. Who is that beautiful young woman your eyes now behold?

Remember back when you had that twinkle in your eye - during Christmas of '85?

That's when things made sense, that's when waking up on Christmas morning and opening presents meant something beyond that beautiful white picket fence.

Look at your family sitting around the fireplace. There he is, his arms outstretched, ready for that warm embrace.

Remember how he used to look at you? Remember how he made you feel when he looked into your soul with those beautiful eyes of blue?

Can you hear it? Can you hear "Silent Night" playing on the record player while he kisses the children goodnight?

"Silent night, holy night.."

"It's time for bed now, Santa's on his way. When you wake up in the morning, you'll have lots of presents - straight from his magical sleigh!"

Remember how you looked at him that night? Do you remember how his face lit up when he smiled back at you in the glow of the Christmas lights?

"All is calm, all is bright..."

The scene plays out in slow motion before your eyes. Suddenly you're reminded of how truly time quickly flies.

Do you remember four toasty bare feet resting in front of the fireplace? Do you remember him tickling your cheek with his shoelace?

Do you remember toasting a glass of eggnog so loudly that Isaac woke up?

"I thought I heard the sound of a sleigh bell!" The little one excitedly announced.

"You'll never know, so you'd best get back to sleep because we'll never tell!" He whispered to them.

"Round yon virgin, mother and child..."

Do you remember that look he gave you when you gave him your last kiss?

Did you ever think that stroking your fingers through his beard would be something you'd one day miss?

"Sleep in heavenly peace.."

No one ever asks for cancer. But we pray and pray and hope for answers.

For a moment you swear you see his face smiling back at you from that vintage silver ball. Hand to your chest, deep breath. Smile. Suddenly he doesn't seem so far away at all.

Sometimes memories are all we have remaining. Sometimes you hear his voice in the middle of the night when it's raining.

Sometimes you feel him wrap his arms around you. You swear you'd seen him in some of the pictures you drew.

Sometimes you don't feel him at all. Sometimes you wonder how much longer you can hold yourself together before you fall.

Sometimes you wake up wondering if this loneliness will persist. Wondering if true happiness truly exists.

But tonight, on the eve of Christmas all those happy memories come back into view.

Your eyes are heavy, your body is weak. A smile returns to your face as you fall peacefully to sleep.

"Sleep in heavenly peace..."

One day our lungs will breathe again. One day our hearts will start beating once more. One day we won't take each other for granted any more. One day our love for each other will be stronger than it's ever been and humanity will continue, it will thrive, and we will begin again. - The Ghosts

Higher

Some might say she's got her head in the clouds. Some might say she's floating on a dream.

But I know the truth.

Some say she's delusional, that she's lost her mind.

But I know her secret.

She figured out what no one else ever could. She figured out what it means to be human. She discovered that it's not the color of one's skin that defines them, not the tone in their voice, not the physical abilities, nor the shape of the body.

She learned to let go. She learned to be herself, embrace her soul, find contentment in the way God made her.

She found her wings, found what inspires her to soar.

She found herself - something most of the world spend their whole lives trying to find.

She discovered she has a soul, and has chosen to love rather than hate, to forgive rather than condemn.

She is love.

And there's nothing more beautiful than that.

The Wolf

The ravenous wolf of time grows hungrier for us every day. Each passing day brings it closer, reminding us of our inevitable mortality.

Plagued with frailty, weakness and the sting of decay, we press on through life's barriers one by one.

Sometimes moving slowly forward through a sea of molasses we keep going, chasing after the dream of a better life, a new start, something real and fresh out that brings happiness to our souls.

And yet the wolf keeps chasing, hungrier and hungrier as each hour passes.

It's a fate we can not seem to escape. The hour of devouring will soon be at hand. Meal time approaches, and the table is set.

Will we make it to the finish line? Will we one day bask in the rays of the warm sunlight, free from harm, pain and sorrow?

Come, wolf. Chase after me. Try and catch me if you can. Always pressing forward, I won't let the foul smell of your breath defeat me. I won't let your intimidating growls shake me. I won't let your claws rip me to shreds when I am down.

I will keep pressing on, through the forest of thorns, over the rivers of sorrows, past the desolate landscapes of the lonely desert, and into the depths of the darkest seas.

And when I've made it home, one day I'll look back on you with a fiery confidence in my eyes, and I'll pull back my bow and fire an arrow into your skull. With a smile, I'll say, "You couldn't catch me. Now I've caught you."

And then I'll stand over your corpse and say, "Thank you for chasing after me all these years. If it wasn't for you, I never would have made it this far."

Societatis

Let the dead hearts rot away.

Hit the reset button again today.

What madness have we embraced?

All our memories have been erased.

Seeking pleasure in a haze of smoke,

Too afraid so we'd rather choke.

What ever happened to facing our fears?

We'd rather pop a bottle and drown in our tears.

Religion has failed us so we seek other means of salvation, hoping for new ways to take our souls to a higher elevation.

Red and blue minds splattered on the pavement, forgetting what democracy truly meant, mad tyrants shaking fists, sheep wallowing in their deceptive shit.

What if we search but never find true peace?

We try to find answers while we helplessly watch the depression increase, but there's no cure for this new disease.

Can meaning be found by cutting the cord?

Can relief be found in empty boxes of cardboard?

Standing in line like lifeless mannequins to start our day, while our bodies wither away into slow decay.

Diving into blue screens, you're oblivious to the world around you. Don't think about what's outside, don't take another step or you'll fall through.

What's out there is too much to bear, so stay inside and remain scared.

Masquerading as a beauty queen for all the world to see, don't let them see the glue that holds you together tightly.

Keep your head held high, pretending it's all ok. Can't let them know you wake up in tears every day.

What is the meaning of your miserable existence? How long before there's no one left to distance?

Billboards paint hopeful messages hidden behind pearl smiles and baby blue eyes, disguising poisons that will lead to your untimely demise.

Seeking blessings from a lost dimension, hoping to achieve some kind of higher ascension.

Where is the truth? Was it lost so long ago in the days of your youth?

Is truth written in the stars, or is it found on the back of magical cards?

Can happiness be found in poison injections, fetus jars or fancy cars?

Do blessings come from nightly rituals? Who can tell the difference between the spiritual and the habitual?

Love and affection are taking a vacation, far away to some unknown location.

Trading beating hearts for nights filled with lust. But in the end all we become is another pile of dust.

What direction is this world spinning? How much longer can we exist if we keep on sinning?

If it's darkness you seek, you'll find it in spades. Look around long enough and you'll find it in plenty of shades.

Yet despite all this I know that there is still hope. It isn't found in blood spilled from slit wrists or a noose made of rope.

It isn't found in little white pills or or at the bottom of aging stills.

If you ask me I'd say that there is only one way.

Only one who paid the price for all of this to go away.

It's too bad the world is too afraid.

Too afraid to believe that there is hope in all this decay.

Too afraid to accept that their hearts beat for a reason. Too scared to believe that for all things there is a season.

Despite what they say, despite what they would have me believe, I know that love is still out there waiting to be received.

Consequences

It wasn't enough for me to see the beauty that was right in front of me.

It wasn't enough for her to lift my broken heart up from the floor.

I wanted more.

And when she gave I took.

Baring her soul to me like an open book, I decided to take a closer look.

And when I saw what had been written, I shook.

A reality I had written fiction about suddenly became so real to me.

A fucked up life covered in other people's shit isn't just a naive boy's fantasy.

So let's skip the pleasantries.

The truth is sinister, ugly and nothing she ever dreamed her life would be.

I saw this clearly, and still I decided to take until her fragile heart started to break.

I squeezed and squeezed until there was nothing left inside, and when she came looking for me to save her, I ran and hid.

I wasn't the man I promised her I'd be.

I believed I was a good man, when all this time there was an asshole hiding inside me.

Like a scared pup I ran from her bleeding body and I fucked it all up.

She needed a tourniquet.

I didn't give a shit.

The hardest thing I've ever done is look into the mirror and admit that I'm not a good son.

I thought I could save the world, give my heart to the needy and stand up for justice.

But in the end I cared for no one.

A handsome face could not hide the demons I so eagerly chased, could not save my integrity from such ugly disgrace.

Now she's gone and there is nothing left for my hungry soul to feed on.

Is the poison of self too strong? Is it too late to save a man as wretched as me?

Perhaps the truth has been there all along.

All I ever had to do was admit that I was wrong.

Rise

I'm so tired of love poems, songs about falling in love, pictures of affection.

I'd rather rip away this wallpaper and tear down these walls to find some kind of meaningful connection.

I was never meant to be trapped by four walls, never destined to spend my life opening and closing doors down endless halls.

I was born to break free from the monotony of the nine to five grind, always destined to become enlightened with truth and expand my mind.

Does the world run on the fuel of affection? If that's the case, I'd rather sever my connection.

I'm a world changer, a head banger, a lion tamer. I'm a powerful train that can't be stopped, a nightmare creeping into your mind at 3 o'clock.

I desire power over love, destruction over hugs.

I demand respect and I'll have it. I'll rise up and save myself from the pit, stepping on other people's shit to reach the top and I'll be damn proud of it.

I belong up there among the stars, not trapped in fancy high rise buildings or bend the wheel of fancy cars.

Some are born for greatness.

I'm a master of this world and one day I'll have the acumen to one day rule it.

What a shame I'm only human.

"Turn back the clock and save some time. Turn it back further to the days when you were mine." — The Ghosts

Sleep in heavenly peace

We used to listen to scary stories told in the dark, designed to give us nightmares and terrify our tiny little hearts.

But no one ever told us that the monsters under our beds would be friendlier than the demons that would live inside our broken heads.

Now we'd run to our nightmares to escape from this cold reality, escape from the world we were promised that isn't what they told us it would be.

I'd rather thumb through the pages of a scary children's book than count more dead bodies and log the hours of the last breaths they took.

Ask the little girl down the street if she believes in ghosts. She'll tell you "no." But she believes in the devil, and he's no Casper, just ask her.

Kids hide under the sheets not from the bogeyman or monsters, but from the bullets and blood ripping through the streets.

I wish I could say our parents taught us well, but nothing they ever could have done would have prepared us for this hell.

We are the midnight society, the broken, the shameful, the wannabes. We are the creepers, the crazies, the shadows they warned us about hiding in the trees.

The world is in our hands now and they say we've got it coming. If our nightmares are our safe place, then we better start running.

No dreams tonight my friends, no trips to slumber land. Better hope and pray we make it through the night, better fold those blessed hands.

I wouldn't jump into bed if I were you, wouldn't hit the hay or catch some shuteye. Because tonight you may never wake, this might be your chance to die.

They say all is calm and all is bright, but I can still hear the demons cackling through the night. It'll take a lamb to save us, a savior to lead us through these twisted mazes.

I never thought we'd become ghosts before we passed, never knew we'd destroy ourselves with all the weapons we'd quickly amassed.

No one ever told us the most terrifying bumps in the night were caused by our own feet, that we were the ones we used to hide from underneath the sheets.

Now we wander like ghosts, afraid to embrace what our souls crave most: our own humanity, lost long ago in the digital memories of our social media posts.

Splat

January 28, 1986:

"Desperate people do crazy things."

The final words spoken by Cynthia before she pulled the trigger that fateful morning.

All it took was one bullet to rip through Gary's skull and penetrate his brain, ending his life with a spray of blood that saturated her sleeve.

It was a night of revelry, filled with liquor and lines of cocaine - typical for the two of them on a weeknight.

Lovers and addicts are all the same. Whether the addiction is a chemical substance or endorphins saturating the brain.

It was jealousy that drove her to pick up the nine millimeter.

Gary's blood flowed like a river onto the linoleum floor. Their cat Muffy, as if completely oblivious to what had happened, stuck her nose down to the blood and took a few sniffs before deciding this substance wasn't something she was interested in tasting.

Before the smell of sulfur had dissipated, Cynthia had already disappeared.

She'd hastily driven away from the scene of the crime, hoping she could get out of town before the cops found out.

As she turned onto the highway, a large spat hit her windshield. It was a mosquito that was filled with human blood.

"Shit! What the hell?"

Cynthia frantically tried using her windshield wipers to scrape it away, but the wipers wouldn't turn.

"You've got to be kidding me!"

Wednesday, 8:30 p.m. Two days before the murder. Gary and Cynthia had finished a big fight in the kitchen over a love note she'd received from another man. Tired of listening to her excuses, Gary decided to grab the dog leash hanging from a hook on the wall.

"I'm taking Muffin for a walk."

"Good," Cynthia murmured. "I hope you don't fucking come back either!"

Walking the dog was a respite from Gary's painful reality with Cynthia. Sure, neither of them were even close to being functional together, but at the end of the day, they knew they couldn't live without each other.

A small mosquito lands on Gary's neck and in a fraction of a second pokes its proboscis into his neck, sucking in a rich drink of his blood.

"Son of a.."

Gary slaps his neck, thinking he's killed it, but the mosquito escapes unscathed with a belly full of crimson sustenance.

Cynthia's trembling hands grasp the steering wheel as she continues down the highway, the blood stain still obscuring her view. She can't stop now. If she did, the cops might see her. They could be on her trail right now.

She couldn't get that blood splatter out of her mind. It was right in front of her, reminding her of what she'd done. Like a bad curse, it stayed with her during the two hour drive south into Sedona.

Finally, she found a secluded hotel in the middle of nowhere and decided to rest.

Thursday, 24 hours before the murder. She wants to leave him. She feels stuck, living in the same house with what feels like a complete stranger. He makes a little money, but just barely enough to get by. He pays for her drugs, which is really the only reason she's still around. She knows about his "secret stash" he keeps on a shelf in the closet. Last time she checked, it was filled with hundred dollar bills, mostly from drug sales.

Cynthia sat in her lonely hotel room, flipping through the wad of cash, closing her eyes as the flipping of the paper sings its rigid tune.

Was it worth it? Did she really have to kill him to get that money? She wouldn't have much time to think.

Suddenly a loud crash occurs outside her window. She looks outside and sees two men breaking into her van.

"Hey! What the hell do you think you're doing?!" She screams at them as she runs out the door in her bathrobe, lit cigarette dangling from her dry lips.

The windshield had been busted into pieces. Glass was strewn all over the sidewalk in front of her hotel room.

"Ouch! Mother fu.."

Cynthia realized she was barefoot. She looked down and saw a piece of glass stuck in her big toe. It was gushing blood.

One year ago. Dr. Hoffman's office.

"Listen, uh...you're not going to tell anyone about this? Right? I mean... my wife, she can't find out."

Gary nervously rubbed his hands together.

"It's ok, Gary. As your doctor I'm not obligated to tell anyone unless it's at your personal discretion."

It was HIV. Probably from a dirty needle. He wouldn't tell Cynthia. He figured he would ride it out and she'd be none the wiser.

"Rock Hudson has done just fine, right doc? This ain't nothing. Life goes on, right?"

It's not like he'd transfer it to her. He and Cynthia hadn't had sex in over two years.

Cynthia yanked out the shard of glass and fell to the ground. It was the worst pain she'd ever felt.

"Holy mother of.."

As she screamed in agony, when her teary eyes cleared for a moment, she realized the piece of glass she pulled out that she was still holding was already stained with blood.

"That damn mosquito! Fucking karma!"

But Cynthia was already doomed. She just didn't realize it yet.

The vandals were already long gone. The van was next to useless now, and she couldn't report it for fear of the police finding her.

As she dragged herself to the motel door, she could hear a buzzing sound from somewhere in the distance.

And that's when it happened.

The next morning, Cynthia's mutilated body was found lying flattened in the parking lot of the motel. Authorities claimed that a massive object had fallen on her from a great height.

At 11:38 a.m. that day, the Challenger space shuttle exploded 73 seconds into flight, killing the lives of all on board. Debris from the shuttle was scattered for miles around the surrounding area.

Cynthia was in the wrong place at the wrong time. Was this mere coincidence, or something more? Divine retribution?

Some secrets aren't meant to be revealed, some mysteries never meant to be solved.

Surgery

Two quick knocks on the door, I find myself in this cold, sterile room once more.

The doctor is in, it's time for the journey to start.

Before I become whole, they must first tear me apart.

Laid open on the table next to the gleaming scalpels and various life saving instruments,

I am asleep, unaware, but the truth of reality sets in.

Not long before on this table laid my wife. She battled so long but she couldn't win the fight. What should have saved her cost her her life.

She was in such better shape than I was, and if it didn't work to save her, why in the world would they want to save my feeble self?

Am I nothing but a lab rat, waiting for the next experimental treatment?

I feel like all eyes are on me like some twisted form of human currency. Except for holding any real worth, I only display value with my every medical emergency

They tell me this cancer is terminal, there is no cure. So why in the world are they trying to save me for?

I already knew the end was near, I wasn't shocked when they gave me less than a year.

However, they wanted to try something new, I had nothing left to lose. But I wasn't aware of what surgery the doctor wanted to do.

Honey, I will see you again soon. I will meet you on the very operating table in which we lost you.

All roads end here don't they? In cold sterile rooms surrounded by faces of those we never knew. Most everyone's final breaths are taken surrounded by beeping machines, such as the ones around me.

The lucky ones pass on before hearing those final two knocks on the door. They pass in their homes, surrounded by those they love and know.

I wasn't one of them, weighed down too heavily by my own sin. I lay on that operating table as I see my wife once again. I feel like I'm drowning, battling the waves. The shocks like eels in the ocean jerking me back to the table before I drift away again.

Whether we sink or swim, death always wins in the end.

Yellow Dress

Yellow dress.

It could have been red, but you chose yellow to capture the heart of a certain fellow.

White ribbon.

It dangles from your ponytail. Your mother smiles as she puts it on while you wonder what type of tux he'd be in.

Little brown purse.

Filled with lipstick tissues and a love letter soaked in perfume. The potent sweet smell danced across your bedroom.

Smile.

Take a last glance in the mirror.

Look out the window and see the headlights as they draw near.

Knock.

You run down the staircase and the sight of him takes your breath away.

And in all the commotion you nearly forget how to walk.

With two smiles and a wave to mom, you hop in his 1957 Chevy.

Your destination? Prom.

As the radio played your favorite song, you blissfully sing along.

Oblivious to the events that were coming, you were lost in his eyes as he showed off to you by drumming.

Who would have thought that life could change in an instant?

Flashing white light.

Here today- tomorrow non- non-existent.

Yellow dress.

Crumbled up on the busted floorboard, stained with the crimson red it could have been.

White ribbon.

Lying under glass in shreds.

Little brown purse.

It's contents scattered across the wet ground, except the bloodstained letter the officer had found.

Smile.

In the cold night air they paced back and forth, trying to identify the remains before them.

A couple of teeth helped them piece it together, but it took them awhile.

Knock.

There was a noise.

Was it possible someone was still alive?

It was his knuckles against the crushed roof.

He may survive if they get to him in time

Tick, tock, tick, tock…

Suddenly it was a race against the clock.

20 years pass and he's sitting in bed, holding onto the old stained letter he had just read.

He'd read it before at least a hundred times for sure.

But no matter how many times he read it, it would never bring the past to present.

He couldn't find a cure for the torture he'd endured.

His hand trembles as he lifts his gun.

He slowly raises it to press it against his mind that had finally come undone.

He could never forgive himself for what happened that night.

He had replayed the scenario a thousand times but try as he may he could never make it right.

Blinding white light.

She smiled in front of him and held out her hand, beckoning that he follow along.

And in her yellow dress and he in his tux, they finally made it to prom.

Among the sleeping

Those old ghosts of yesterday, where did they go? All those memories: were they real?

When you're left alone with your thoughts, you notice things that some may take for granted.

The crickets still play their evening symphony, just as they always have. But something's missing. Maybe it's the howling of the wind through the trees. Maybe it's the croaking of the frogs or the ominous hooting of the owls.

Or maybe it's the sound of your voice.

My vision's a little blurrier these days. Maybe it's because the future is harder to see now without you in it.

We were supposed to settle down together in this cabin, surrounded by these snowy peaks and rising timbers. We promised no matter what happened we'd fight to make this work, use every last ounce of strength to hold the weight of the world on our shoulders.

But then he came.

And then you left.

Now shifting shadows are my only company, memories of yesterday my only friends.

If the rain stopped there'd be no more tears left to cry. If the sun burned out the infernal anger inside our hearts would be extinguished.

They say there's life after love. No one told me my world would turn into a living hell after losing you.

It feels like I've died, but instead of moving on the entire world moved on without me.

I feel like a ghost, screaming in the atmosphere but no one can see or hear me. My flesh passed away with my heart the day you decided to walk away. All those stories I wrote for you, all those words I carefully pieced together from my heart were taken with you when you walked out the door.

As you exited through the door that fateful night, a new one opened up for me.

And then another.

And another.

But no one could ever love the way you did. No one could touch me the way you did, look into my eyes with that magical glow, whisper into my ear in the middle of the night that I was your everything. So as those doors opened, I kept closing them.

There's only one door I want to see open again - the same one you walked out of five years ago.

There's nothing left for me out there, no reason to move forward, no ambition left to climb new mountains, no drive to build new castles or create new memories with someone.

I'd rather stay here. I'd rather fade away into these cabin walls, become one with nature as it overtakes this empty, decaying vessel once filled with rays of hope.

Some day they'll find my rotting corpse sitting here in this chair, still facing the front door, waiting for you to come back home.

But what they won't realize is that this man died long before his body began to decay, long before his anguished soul exited one prison only to escape to an eternal one.

I hope you've found your happy ending. One of us deserves that, at least.

So I'll embrace my somber fate.

I will find my place among the sleeping, and dream of a life that should have been.

Sunken Treasure

Ancient treasures buried so deep,

Resting silently while the world above sleeps;

Memories sunken below the waves,

Whisper tales of brighter days from the fearless and the braves.

Centuries have passed since we've seen you last;

Scattered around a broken old mast.

What secrets does golden visage hide?

So many memories tucked away inside.

Soaked in salt water, wrapped in seaweed,

Strewn about on the ocean floor like a book to read.

Look closely and find the truth, an ancient tale of squandered youth.

Even now these ghosts teach us to fight the greed and to fight the lust.

No matter the depth, the message remains the same: whenever we are

lost, sometimes it's better to go back from whence we came.

One day these nuggets of truth will rise again.

And a new day filled with wisdom shall begin.

Light up Ahead

"Take this heart of darkness, I give it up..."

2004, summer. My finger touches the play button on my car stereo, and track one starts playing on Further Seems Forever's latest album "Hide Nothing."

It's a warm summer day and "Light up Ahead" is cranked up loudly as the AC blows directly into my face.

The song, to me, was an uplifting one. The lyrics were full of inspiration to keep moving forward, that no matter how dark and grim or complicated life gets, there's always a light at the end of the tunnel. It was an empowering song that toasted to the personal strength we draw from when we feel there is nothing left.

This album could be categorized as "Christian rock," which admittedly I immersed myself into in those days. Record label Tooth and Nail cranked out a new Christian rock album seemingly every month, and I was there to snatch up every one I could get my hands on.

There I was, driving down the road rocking out to some inspirational Christian rock song, feeling inspired and uplifted as lead singer Jon Bunch's voice screamed out with unwavering passion for what I perceived as absolute truth.
"It gets so complicated if you live enough, turn into what you hated, you're breaking up.."

I always liked that verse. For me it reminded me that life can take some pretty dark turns sometimes, and the older we get, the more complicated life becomes and that innocence we once hung on to slowly fades away, but there's always hope waiting at the end of the line, when we feel lost and alone.

I decided to park my car at a nearby park and eat the spicy chicken sandwich I just picked up from Burger King. I roll the windows down and let the warm breeze in, and as I take my first bite, Jon continues, "And all these bad dreams, I wake up to the light.."

"Wake me up.."

Fast forward to 2016, somewhere in California,
Jon Bunch's lifeless body was found in his car. He was discovered in his car, which was parked in a church courtyard. Jon was still wearing his Trader Joe's work uniform and a name tag that said "Jon B." on it.

The coroner would later reveal that Jon's death was via suicide from an overdose of sleeping pills.

"There's a light up ahead..." or so I had thought.

When I heard the news, my heart sank. I'd long since moved on from Christian rock, and had embraced a taste for indie rock and metal. I had all but forgotten about Further Seems Forever, and it seemed to me that maybe Jon's fans had too.

"Trader Joe's? How does a guy go from being a front man of a highly popular band to working at Trader Joe's?" I couldn't help but wonder what he was doing in that church parking lot. Was he trying to reach out to God one last time? Had he fallen away from his purpose in life?

All I could feel was deep sadness. Twelve years ago this guy was touching my heart in the deepest of ways with the sound of his voice, inspiring me to keep moving forward and never give up.

And now he's gone, he had taken his own life. Just like that, it seemed like the hope he had been singing about all those years ago had been snuffed out somehow.

What happened, Jon?

I may never know the answers as to why he did it, but as Don McClean's song "The day the music died," for me that was the day that Christian rock music died. The candle of passion that had burned lower and lower as I moved to different genres was effectively snuffed out.

Fast forward two years later and I'm on the phone with the lead singer of a Christian rock band I loved called Project 86. Through a Kickstarter campaign, I had the unique opportunity to spend an hour on the phone with a guy that I more or less idolized in the Christian rock scene for many years.

Soon we found ourselves in a deep discussion about Christian rock artists and the extreme amount of pressure they go through, all because of a label they're given.

"It's like you're constantly under a microscope," he told me. "It's completely unrealistic to live up to the perceived expectations some fans have for you, and sometimes that pressure becomes too much."

He explained that under "Christian" labels, if band members veered too far in the "wrong" direction, they instantly became demonized and shunned for being "too sinful." Project 86 continues to thrive because they aren't recognized as a Christian band any more.

"I'm still a Christian, but I learned a long time ago that having that Christian label on the band hurt us more than anything," He told me.

Maybe that's what happened to Jon. Maybe the pressure of having to be this squeaky clean, goody two shoes guy was just too much to handle. The pressure to behave as the "Christian" demographic expects is

I couldn't blame him if that was the case. In 2004 if I'd been caught with the tattoo sleeves I currently have, I probably would have been labeled a Satan worshipper. The world back then was much more judgmental, and less accepting than even the world today.

Jon's death made me question myself and how much faith I had put into flawed human beings just like me who were placed upon pedestals and forced to behave in a completely unrealistic manner, weighed down by expectations that no human being could live up to.
Was I guilty of hero worship? Did I contribute to that kind of religious nonsense?

Christian music was everything to me back then. I lived it, breathed it. I fell for the hype and believed that somehow I was more righteous than my brothers and sisters who were listening to that awful "secular music."
Today I look back on that era of my life and I'm extremely ashamed of who I was.

I'm not entirely sure I wouldn't have been a contributor to the judgmental, so-called "justified anger" that so many Christians felt back then toward anything that was deemed secular or "of the world." That's a sobering thought for sure.

I had a lot to learn back then, and thank God I figured out that I'm a sinner just like everyone else, with flaws and sinful thoughts and desires and hopes and dreams like my fellow brothers and sisters in this world.

I guess I never really liked that quotation that was pounded into our young Christian minds that says "be in the world but not of the world," because I'm always going to be of the world, since last time I checked I'm a human being that was born on the same planet as everyone else.

I get what they were trying to convey with that quote, and furthermore what the Bible has to say about it, but the Jesus I know would love everyone not because they're on a pedestal, not because they sing in a fancy rock band or make millions of dollars on record sales.
The Jesus I know would simply love.

I don't know what Jon was going through when he overdosed on those sleeping pills. That's something only he and God know.

The one thing I do know though, is that even after 17 years, Jon's voice still brings truth and hope to those who hear it, whether he is still here or not.
The lesson I learned was that even though the world seems dark sometimes and things seem bleak, the message of hope remains.

Jon was human just like anyone else. Jon lived and died as a man who faced temptations and heartache just like me or anyone else has. He had flaws and strengths, but because he was in the spotlight he had to deal with so much more pressure. Enough to crush even the strongest diamonds.

But his voice lives on forever, on an album that is filled with truth, hope and most importantly, love. Love that continues to spread into the hearts of the broken, the lost, and the searching.

Maybe Jon didn't feel hope or feel loved when he took his own life. Maybe he did. Whatever the case may be, hope and love were always there, and always will be. Not just for him, not just for me, but for everyone on the planet.

I can't think of anything more human than trying.
I can't think of anything more human than giving up.
And human is all I'll ever be.
But the light up ahead will always be there, whether I'm succeeding or giving up.

Jon taught me that, and I'm forever grateful to him for showing me that no matter how dark life gets, hope is still there. There is, and will always be a light up ahead, and it is worth fighting for.

Academic Days

I left all my memories back in 2005, when I was still learning how to survive.

We met in college, sparking romance on the world's stage. Before you life had been meaningless, until you helped me turn the page.

We slept together, embraced underneath the sheets trying to figure out how to make our lice's complete.

Binging on junk food for days and days, "Good Times" marathons in the month of May, doing what we could to make our own way.

So young and innocent, we wondered where the years had gone. Little did we know that the years ahead would be twisted and bent.

It was a year of crossroads, hard lessons and watching our friends pass on while the alcohol flowed.

It was the final year of true freedom, before life hit us hard and took away the keys to our beautiful kingdom.

Responsibility? Who knew. Just another brick in the wall, another issue to ignore until life shoved it into view.

Were we happy or just faking it? You and I were so lost in passion and pleasure, we never wanted to quit.

So many different shades your panties painted on the floor, so many times we sinned behind my locked bedroom door.

As the walls began to decay, as life pushed us forward and took our fun away, we both were forced to grow up and go our separate ways.

Funny how we grow up and memories fade. Life changes so quickly day by day.

We split up so long ago and what we had long ago died, but sometimes I wonder how life had been if we had never said goodbye.

Life is quite different now, I'm sure you'd agree. One of us found happiness while the other is wondering how his life turned out to be so shitty.

Now I'm sure you're lying in bed with him after a night of pleasure while I'm lying motionless still dreaming of finding life's greatest treasure.

Sometimes in my mind I rewind the clock back to our time, remembering the smiles we shared, all those mountains we would climb.

Some say experience is everything. Someday wisdom is more meaningful than rushing in with a diamond ring.

If this is true, I'm thankful to have walked away not empty handed, but with my heart and mind expanded.

It wasn't the academic lessons that shaped me into who I am today. It was the memories you and I made that molded me into a man in so many ways.

Whatever the future may hold for us, whether success or harm, I'm thankful for the many nights I held you tightly in my arms.

Those academic days taught me so many things.

Isn't it amazing how much positive change a college romance can bring?

Disintegrate

"I'm sorry, I just… don't want this anymore," she told me, then told me to leave the coffee shop where we'd had our first date, our first kiss, our first moment of love.

After two years of pure bliss, passionate lovemaking and countless nights snuggling on the couch, she decided to end it. Just like that. No real explanation, just a few words was all it took to seal the deal.

"There's no logic in this."

I rose to meet her eye to eye, in hopes that I would see some flicker of affection left. But there was none.

She stopped and looked at me incredulously. Silent, looking ashen. When had her skin paled so much?

That's all I said though. I wanted to say a lot more, but to be honest, at that point I'd given my last damn with failed relationships. So I turned my back on her and walked out the door.

"Wait!"

I faintly heard her call out as I left. It didn't matter. I didn't matter to her anymore, so she'd get no more of my time.

I went home that night and analyzed the situation. I drew the conclusion that things just didn't make sense anymore. I looked back at how it was in the beginning, how everything seemed so right, but in recent months it seemed the more sense things made, the more she became detached.

In the days that followed, I spent every waking moment glued to the screen of my phone, hoping and praying that I would get something from her, despite my not looking back. And as I watched her Facebook wall filled with pictures of her smiling and having good times out with friends, my heart sank more and more.

Frustrated, and angry as hell, I threw my phone across the room, watching it hit the wall and shattering like a porcelain doll hitting pavement.

"Fuck this, I'm getting out of here."

I took one look outside and saw rain pouring down onto the cold streets, but didn't care. I threw on a worn hoodie and headed out the door.

My destination?

Didn't matter. Just had to go somewhere other than that tiny, cold apartment.

I walked the streets for ten minutes or so, brooding over the stupid choices and selfish mistakes I'd made over the last two years, which then led to tangent thoughts of all the mistakes I had ever made in any relationship.

"Forget it. Forget her, and forget being with anyone. I don't need to be with anyone to make me happy," I thought. I knew the words were true, but I didn't feel their affirmative meanings yet. I'd made up my mind that the world could go fuck itself, and relationships were for fools. So I kept walking, looking down and watching my cold breath form in front of me.

By the time I hit the downtown plaza where my favorite pizza joint sat, Phlan's Pizza, I was soaked from head to toe.

"Ok, this was a stupid idea. Maybe I better find a nice place to dry off," I thought, thinking of going in for a slice.

Then I heard it. A voice coming from a nearby alleyway behind me.

"Sir, may we have a moment of your time please?" A female voice echoed through the brick walls of the darkened alley. It was enticing, seductive almost. I was done with seductive voices though, they never seemed to stick around long.

I positioned myself under an awning and lifted my hood up. Standing in front of an old rusty metal door was a man and woman, seemingly dressed up for a night out. "Hey, you look like you could use a good drying off, my friend," the man told me.

These two people though, their faces...something wasn't quite right about them. Maybe it was the rain, maybe it was the dark night, or maybe I wasn't quite as sober as I thought I was, but at first glance, they both had this weird grin on their faces, almost like a forced smile.

I stepped into the light of the doorway and suddenly the couple simultaneously grabbed me and forced me into a large open room that looked a lot like a church sanctuary. But there were no religious symbols to be found anywhere.

The couple sat me down in the middle of the sanctuary on a pew surrounded by other couples. In fact, upon closer inspection, it appeared that I was the only "single" person in the room. Everyone in the room was with someone. All the men had their arms around their women, and every single one of them had that weird forced grin on their faces.

Before I could even try to make sense of what on earth was going on, the piano music started playing and a man dressed in a fine suit stepped onto the stage.

"I want to welcome you all this evening to this fine service, and it's really good to see all your beautiful smiling faces!" he loudly proclaimed.

Now, let's kick things off with a hymn, shall we?"

He then directed us to turn in our "hymnals" to page 234, a song called "Engine 45." Everyone rose to their feet in unison. The woman sitting next to me grabbed my arm and forced me to stand up with the rest of them. She handed me a hymnal and I looked down at it, taking a deep breath and then swallowing hard.

"All my life, I've been waiting for something that never came..." they sang. Before the song finished, the "preacher" interrupted.

"Brothers and sisters, I know you've all been through a lot during your dark days of being single, but I'm here to tell you tonight that there is POWER in being together! There's pleasure in being a couple! And do you remember what I have told you many times before? What have I told you about how to speak to your significant other? Turn in your hymnals to page 124 and let's find out!"

The next song began with an eerie tune, something beautifully broken..

"..And I'll use you as a warning sign, that if you talk enough sense then you'll lose your mind..."

Those words rang through my mind and pierced my brain like a dagger. For a moment my vision got blurry and the music distorted a bit. I started to feel anxious, my heart started racing and I could feel sweat starting to trickle down my forehead. It seemed really hot in that sanctuary, and the air was heavy, making it hard for me to breathe.

Suddenly, I felt a tap on my shoulder. I looked to my left and saw the woman sitting next to me holding out what appeared to be a Bible.

"Take it," she whispered. Her face had begun to take on similar characteristics of everyone else in the room, as though all their faces were becoming the same face.

I sat there for a moment and didn't respond, my head still ringing from the music being played.

"TAKE IT!" She screamed into my face, her eyes filled with blackness and her gaping smile stretched further across her face.

I grabbed the book and looked down at it. The book had no distinguishing features from the outside, but it was thick and heavy.

I opened it up and to my disbelief, all the books included in it were the names of my exes. Before I could take it in, the preacher interrupted my thoughts again, this time his voice was louder than the woman next to me.

"NOW LET'S TURN TO THE BOOK OF CASSANDRA, CHAPTER 24: VERSE 13!" He shouted. The woman next to me grabbed the Bible I was holding from my hands and turned to the passage. It read:

"He who boasts about being with a woman, may he take heed, for neglecting her needs and focusing on his own wants and desires will lead to certain destruction."

Cassandra.

My fourth girlfriend in high school. The words on the page directly correlated with what happened between us. Back then, I was a selfish jerk who threw my status around as a "taken man" just to make myself seem more popular. In doing so I had neglected her, and things fell completely apart.

What was going on here? How did they...how did they know?

"The next passage we need to take to heart is Audrey 22: 12-19," the preacher announced, landing his cold gaze on me. He proceeded to read a passage about how a man needs to put his significant other first, another lesson I failed to learn from my relationship with Audrey in 2008.

"Selfishness is the work of the evil one!" He shouted. On and on, he read scripture after scripture, as I sat there in a paralytic state, unable to move from my seat. Woman after woman, lessons from the past I failed to heed began to pile up on my brain like a load of steel beams weighing down heavily on me.

I turned my head to look around the room, which somehow seemed to grow bigger with each passing moment, and saw what seemed like hundreds of couples holding hands and smiling, looking so content. And there I was, the lowly single man, the guy who had his chances and blew them over and over again. An overwhelming feeling of guilt welled up inside me. Instantly, everything I had ever done wrong was being exposed for the entire world to see. My heart felt like it was being ripped out of my chest. I couldn't breathe.

"What good is a man, if he has to walk this life ALONE like a FOOL?"

Another hit to the gut. If I was the one making all the mistakes in the relationships, How could

I ever find myself worthy to walk with someone through life?

"Take this man right here for example. Everyone, look at him! Take a look at what the lost looks like!"

I felt a thousand eyes gazing upon me. I began to tremble uncontrollably. Never mind the analysis, the room was getting too creepy. I felt I needed to turn my efforts more toward survival.

"You, sir, have fucked up!" The preacher shouted, staring directly into my eyes with a convicting gaze. "Now it's time to take your worthless soul away and replace it with the happiness that only a relationship can provide!"

A man to my right and the woman to my left then grabbed me and dragged me to the front of the sanctuary. Unable to move on my own, I seemed to have lost control of all movement at this point so I was helpless as they dragged me forward.

Then they threw me down at the altar.

"We are all lost, son, but we need to find the truth to set us free! And to find the truth, you must turn around!"

I regained control of myself and turned around to find the entire congregation standing behind me. Their eyes were black as night and their grins stretched so far across their faces that their cheeks were bleeding. They were all holding hands, but their hands looked like they had fused together, leaving only one arm free for each of them.

One by one they approached me, forcing me to the floor and started digging their fingernails into my skin and ripping it to pieces. Tormented with the most agonizing pain imaginable, I was helpless as they tore me apart while they sang a hymn in unison.

"Sometimes we have to watch our whole lives fall apart before we can rebuild them again!" They shouted over and over again as I felt my body being torn limb from limb.

Then I blacked out.

When I awoke, I found myself lying in my bed.

"A dream. Thank God it was a dream," I mumbled, sweat pouring down my face.

It was dark, so I reached over to the lamp on my nightstand and turned it on.

To my shock, when the light illuminated the room there was a woman lying next to me.

"What the hell just happened? What's going on?"

I slowly reached my hand out to tap her on the shoulder, but when my finger connected to her skin, she suddenly disintegrated into a pile of dust.

I hadn't been asleep, had I? All of it was real.

The room felt hot. Too hot.

Suddenly the room started closing in on me.

My eyes went blurry, and when they readjusted, I could see myself surrounded by tiled walls.

I stood up, dizzied and confused.

"Where...am I?"

An overwhelmed sadness suddenly came over me.

I started to cry. Tears flooded out of my eyes like waterfalls.

I couldn't stop. The tears burst from my eyes into a watery explosion around my face, engulfing my nostrils. I couldn't breathe. I panicked and tried to stop the water. I put my hands over my eye sockets to try and stop it, but the water kept coming. The small room started filling up with water. I would surely soon meet my watery grave.

I held my breath, and accepted my fate.

Darkness.

Silence.

And then I put down my pen.

"I wish it wouldn't take death to make you realize that life is still worth living." – The Ghosts

Returned

Behold the newlywed, so frail but so beautiful. Finally escaped her life behind a depressing cubicle.

A handsome young man she met at church asked her to marry him, but little did she know of his contemplated sin.

Her hair, so beautiful and soft, once blowing in the breeze, now buried six feet under in a state of rot.

Above the grave the night sky is filled with lightning. But down below, her dreadful corpse is quite frightening.

A bolt of lightning strikes the tombstone, the earth shakes and cracks open as she begins to moan.

Her bony fingers clasp at the mud, once less brittle and filled with crimson blood.

Upward she climbs out of her permanent resting place, now she'll have revenge when next she sees his face.

With a crack of the knee-bone she stands up tall, still in her wedding gown moans, "I'm coming for you, my dear Paul!"

Tonight she will have her bittersweet revenge. Tonight's the night he will feel the knife pierce his flesh again and again.

That coward will pay for taking such sweet love from her heart, and using it for his own pleasure, which is not very smart.

As the sky lights up with electricity, she slowly drags her feet into the city.

The rain begins to pour and the thunder claps louder. Tonight hearts are going to explode like gunpowder.

There's his house, she knows it by heart. There in the driveway he proposed to her and promised her a fresh start.

She peers through the window sill with the one eye that remains, and sees him on the couch, sitting with Jenny Romaine.

She scratches the window to the living room, contemplating how Paul will meet his doom.

"If I had any teeth I'd bite into his flesh, and rip his neck apart with a violent thrash."

There he sits on the couch with a grin, but soon his face will be separated from his chin.

The next morning the police found his body. It had been ripped to shreds by something or somebody.

His girlfriend had fled but not without a scratch. Before the night was over she'd screamed and bled.

The only piece of evidence was a bloodied diamond ring, once a symbol of hope and love, now just a meaningless thing.

The young bride on that night got even, took revenge for the night she'd been beaten.

Paul was no more, just a pile of guts on the floor.

The bride would live on, never finding her soulmate, but crept along searching for others who had broken their vows made.

And when she found them there would be hell to pay. Be careful you aren't unfaithful, or you too will end up her prey.

Vows

"The secret of a happy marriage is finding the right person. You know they're right if you love to be with them all the time."—Julia Child

You're just in time for today's special event. Look up on the stage. The couple is about to read their vows. Won't you take a seat?

The couple stare into each other's eyes before a crowd filled with family and friends:

He: I promise to love you all the days ahead, through sickness and in health, for better or for worse. I promise to always be by your side no matter what.

She: I promise to hate you every time there's an argument, and put all the blame on you. I promise to resent you when you become ill, and I'll walk away from you when things start to get rough because I don't care enough to fight for us.

She: I promise that I'll be faithful to you always. You are my one and only, and always will be. I will share our bed with no other. No one could ever take your place.

He: I promise that when I get tired of your body I will seek another's touch; I'll sneak behind your back and fuck every woman I can, to satisfy my own selfish desires. You're always going to be expendable.

He: I will always treat you as a gentleman should treat a lady. I will hold doors open for you, always put you first in everything that I do, and nothing will ever come between you and I.

She: I'll take for granted your kindness and I'll use you for your money, manipulate you into giving me what I want and I'll step all over your heart to fulfill my own wishes. When you try to open doors for me I'll slam them in your face. I'll put my desires before your own, always.

She: I promise to always put God at the center of our relationship always, and let Him lead and guide us in the happiest marriage imaginable. We will worship Him together and through His love we will grow closer to each other every day.

He: I will always whine and complain on Sunday mornings, refusing to help get the kids ready for church. Who needs church? Who needs God? There is only us. We've got this. We'll make this whatever we want it to be. There's no place for ancient superstition in this marriage.

He: I promise I'll never leave you. I've finally found you, my love. After waiting my whole life I've finally found my soulmate. We are truly meant to be united by God above. I would never abandon you or walk away without reason.

She: When I can't handle life's obstacles, I'll question whether we are meant to be. I will curse at God and wonder why I thought He brought us together in the first place. You'll wake up one day and I'll be long gone, with no explanation at all.

She: I promise to meet you at the altar and profess my love for you before God and man. I will make that commitment and keep it.

He: I promise not to show up on our wedding day, instead choosing to get drunk by the river, tossing my damn ring into the water, cursing you at the top of my lungs.

She: "Honey, I can't wait to marry you. We've got so much to look forward to."

He: "This is truly the best decision we could ever make. I'm so in love with you."

And so it begins…

Reflect

The moonlight shines through the bedroom blinds. Your beautiful face illuminates before me.

I gently place my arms around you and pull you closer. Our warm bodies touch, and my breath is taken away.

I take a deep breath, we smile at one another and our lips gently meet.

Passionate kisses spark feelings like fireworks;

You place your hand on my chest and gently slide it downward.

For a moment, you hesitate.

"No. Not this time," you think.

You hold me tighter and hold me closer and drink more deeply from my lips.

One beautiful moment leads to another.

Suddenly you remember the last words he spoke to you:

"Look at you! You're disgusting! You've let yourself go!"

You slowly start to push me away. Suddenly you see a mental picture of your body, those visible stretch marks and cellulite covering your thighs.

You realize you're not young and pretty anymore. Your prime has passed.

"Oh god, what am I doing here? I'm a mess. He doesn't find me attractive."

You begin to panic, but before I can ask you what's wrong, you take a deep breath and pretend like everything is ok.

"It...it's ok honey, I'm fine."

But it's not ok. You know it, and I can sense it.

"Honey, it's ok. We don't have to do this," I whisper softly into your ear.

But in your mind, you know you've blown the moment, and you blame yourself. Now it's too late and you can't go back. The night is ruined.

You turn your head away from me. But then I put my hand gently on your cheek and direct your eyes into mine.

"It's ok. Everything is fine. There's nothing to worry about. Not anymore," I assure you.

You hear my words, but don't believe them.

"They're only words," you figure. "How could he look at me and find beauty in this broken body?"

Time suddenly freezes.

You're faced with a decision. Do you trust him, or do you believe your own lies?

Do you believe what a broken man in your past told you? That You weren't good enough for anyone? That you're worthless? That you're a nasty whore?

Or do you trust the man in front of you, the man who has held you in his arms all night without a single mention of your outward appearance, your inability to love or your lack of compassion?

Are you going to let your ex win? Are you going to give in to him again? After all you've endured, after all the pain he caused you? You remember how hard it was to escape that hell, how long it's taken for those scars to finally start to heal.

"NO! Not anymore! Never again!"

You fight it. You fight the pain, the tears, the anger.

You're better than this. You're better than him. He doesn't own you. He can never hurt you again.

So you close your eyes, take a deep breath and take a step toward me. You slowly wrap your arms around me.

"Everything ok?" I whisper.

"Yeah, everything is great. And you know what? It's going to be great from now on."

You smile at me as the moonlight reflects off your beautiful eyes.

Our passionate connection resumes. Outside, the wind picks up and howls through the window panes, the swaying trees dance in tandem with our body language.

"Wow."

I am completely in awe of you. Nothing could ever change that. No obstacle, no argument, no tears, no painful memories, not even the physically ravaging effects of time. You'll always appear to me a goddess, as radiant as the day I first saw you.

Our warm bodies hit the soft bed and our souls connect once again. Two hearts dancing in the moonlight together - a harmony of passion echoes into the night.

That's you and I, making love on a warm summer evening. That's us, making beautiful memories together. With each passionate kiss, each sigh, we draw closer, not only in body but in spirit.

And when we are finished, I hold you in my arms and whisper in your ear, "I love you."

And as we fall asleep together, we smile, knowing that after so many years of emptiness, we found each other. And no matter what happened before, no matter the pain either of us has experienced in the past, our beautiful love for one another will carry us through countless more passionate nights.

The mask

It's been sitting on my mantle ever since that night.

That night I'll never forget.

It was an evening filled with fancy dresses, dapper tuxedos and colorful facades- a masquerade of the bizarre, the mysterious.

I walked onto the ballroom hidden behind the cover of my plague doctor mask, scoping out potential dance partners.

As the band played louder, she appeared seemingly out of nowhere. Her long, white dress, that beautiful curly brunette hair flowing down her shoulders, and that mask with the pouty red lips on it and rosy cheeks.

"Hello, handsome. You look like you could use some company."

My heart began to race. I held my hand out and our fingers embraced.

The band struck up a beautiful symphony that echoed off the beautifully ordained walls.

As we waltzed together, her hair seemed to sway to the rhythm of the violin. Like ocean waves, her dress flowed with the soothing sounds of the haunting strings.

"You seem to know your way around a dance floor,"

I told her.

"I've had practice," she replied. "It feels like we've danced before."

There was a familiarity about her. I couldn't quite place it.

And then I placed my hand on her hip, moving in closer.

"I don't think I want this night to ever end," I whispered.

"Maybe you'll get your wish, my dear," she said as I saw her right eye wink at me through the mask.

Suddenly a loud pop echoed through the ballroom, followed by a scream.

"Pop. Pop. Pop."

People began to panic, screams echoed off the walls, masks fell to the floor as clueless spectators looked around the room, trying to figure out where the shots were coming from.

"Get down!" I shouted at my nameless dance partner. We hit the floor, forgetting to take our masks off in the panic.

And then, as the crowd began to scatter I saw him.

He was wearing a blue sequined suit and a red harlequin mask.

My heart was racing as I held onto her tightly.

Suddenly the room became silent.

I could hear her heart beating louder as she shivered in my arms.

Then I heard footsteps.

Clack.

Clack.

Clack.

He must have been close. The footsteps became louder and louder.

Then silence again.

"Sit up."

His voice sounded slightly muffled behind the mask.

Terrified to speak, I slowly sat up.

As I looked up I found the barrel of a pistol staring at me. My vision blurred as I contemplated my fate.

Then I heard something hit the floor in front of me. I looked down nervously, and it was his mask.

Sweat began to pour from my head.

And then I saw his face.

He...was me.

It was my own face staring back at me.

"Say goodnight."

Boom.

The bullet pierced my skull and everything went black.

When I woke up, I found myself sitting in front of a fireplace. On the mantle above it rested a harlequin mask.

The night would repeat endlessly.

It was the night I never wanted to end.

Growing Old

Heaven forbid these butterflies ever fly away.

What if we wake up one day to find that we can no longer sway?

Everything we hold so dear is waiting for us right here. But will we feel the same way in 50 years?

What if the lovemaking isn't what it is today?

When such pleasure is gone, will we still endeavor to seize each day?

Love is strong but time's inevitable push threatens to leave us cold and empty.

How will we find new ways to keep things fresh, even when our bones deteriorate and the ravages of age remold our flesh?

I hope we'll never forget to kneel down and pray, to count our blessings one by one each and every day.

If I ever fail to show you how much you truly mean, I hope you'll remember that you will always be my life, my love, my one true queen.

If you ever find distance between yourself and I, I hope that even in our golden years you'll have known that I've always been your guy.

For us, it's not too late, my dear. We're still young, there's no time to wait.

This day is ours and there's so much time ahead for us, so many chapters left to be written, so much good conversation we've yet to discuss.

Let's break the mold and be an example of what true love can be, show the world that love doesn't fade, but only grows stronger as we grow old.

Let every day we live be a reflection of what true love can give, showing the world what it means to forget and forgive. And when we are gone and our journey is through, because of how we lived generations will discover the secret we knew, the key to unlocking a heart's rusted door, and finding and holding onto true love not just for a moment, but forevermore.

"I'm standing next to you on a sandy shore, the past tickling our feet once more. So many years have passed us by, so many tears that we've wiped dry." – The Ghosts

War

"Ok honey, I'll see you soon. I love you."

Maria Delgado hangs up the phone and wipes her cheese broccoli-caked fingers onto her apron.

She's feeding her infant son in his high chair at the kitchen table. The doorbell sounds.

Who could it be at this hour? She wasn't expecting anyone.

She peers through her living room window through the curtain. She sees a black Packard parked by the curb.

Her hands start shaking as she turns the doorknob.

The door opens.

Standing before her is a stranger dressed in a military uniform.

"I'm sorry, Mrs…"

Her right hand presses to her lips as they begin to quiver. Tears begin streaming down her cheeks.

"Oh god, no!" She screams.

She collapses to the floor.

A trench somewhere in Southern France, 1944.

It's been a long day of fighting. No sleep in three days, rations are low, and he's starving. Another rat scurries across his foot, the scent of death hangs everywhere.

"Break time!" The commanding officer shouts.

Break time means mail time on Thursdays. And every week he'd anticipate a letter from his wife back home. He hadn't heard from her in over two months, but each time he eagerly anticipated something from her.

"Looks like your lucky day, Captain," Corporal Manning says as he hands a dusty letter to the weary love-struck soldier.

The thought of hearing from her again almost makes him forget about the same beef stew ration he was about to force down his throat for the twelfth night in a row. Immediately he tears into it, hands shaking so much he can barely keep the unfolded letter steady as he begins to read it. As he reads, his smile slowly fades to shock and his hands steady.

"She...left me," He mumbles. "My god, I can't believe this..."

The note stated that she had indeed left him - for someone else. A mechanic named Frank.

With a look of shock still in his eyes, Captain James Delgado slowly rises to his feet, crumples the note in his left fist, and climbs out of the trench.

"James! What the hell are you doing?" Screams Corporal Manning. "James! James! Jesus, There's live gunfire up there!"

But Captain Delgado doesn't hear the cries of his friend. As bullets whiz past his head, he slowly walks forward, one step at a time, staggering towards enemy fire.

And for a moment he stands there motionless, with a blank stare on his face.

A bullet pierces his shoulder. Then another grazes his cheek bone.

Then the fatal bullet comes that ends Captain Delgado's life, piercing the right side of his brain as he falls lifelessly to the ground, fist still clenching the letter.

For Captain Delgado, the war was over.

He died on the battlefield not as a hero, but as a broken man.

In love and war, it's all the same. Hearts break, dreams shatter. Lives are torn apart and families broken.

Love is a battlefield where no one ever wins. And no one ever knows why they're fighting.

Nothing ends a human life more quickly than love. We'd do anything for it.

We'd even die for it.

Digital Relapse

Somewhere in the digital sea rests conversations of our past, memories we made over late night chat sessions so many years ago.

Echoes of our hopes and fears still pass through electric synapses, tangled up in a virtual web.

If I could somehow dive into that electric landscape and find what we said to one another, I'd find a way to bring it back. I'd find that part of you that's been missing all these years, the part of you that you left inside that silicon jungle, and bring you back to the woman that I fell in love with so long ago.

Before the cold winters of reality chilled your bones, before hot summer nights made you swim in the sweat of your crippling anxiety, before the rapping of the tree branches scratching your bedroom window panes kept you up at night, you and I were floating together on the waves of deep thoughts, sailing on the winds of long distance heart-to-hearts, and discovering new things about ourselves together on islands of cyberspace adventure.

But on that fateful night our connection was suddenly severed. Reality had been seeping into your life too much, and it was wearing you down. I tried reaching out to you, assured you everything was going to be ok. And as much as you cherished our conversations, you couldn't commit any longer to our adventures. Over time your digital escape became more infrequent. For hours each night I'd sit and stare at my computer screen, waiting for you. But you never came.

And when the post came by your sister on social media that you'd taken your own life that night, I didn't want to believe it.

I still don't believe it. Because you're still out there in the digital world, waiting for me. Waiting for us to be reunited.

So I'll find you. I'll enter cyberspace and follow your digital footprints until they lead me back to you. I'll do whatever it takes to fix this broken connection between us.

Amissa Caritate

November afternoon. Leaves rustled across our feet.

You called me up, asked if we could meet.

Arrived in my car, got out of it and saw you standing at the front door.

I didn't realize just how beautiful you really were.

Those beautiful blue eyes, my breath taken away in an instant, such a pleasant surprise.

Your short blonde hair blowing in the wind.

That was the day that you and I first sinned.

Your clothes are lying on the bedroom floor.

You looked at me with those hungry eyes, you wanted more.

My hand on your chest, moving downward.

Eyes locked on mine, we pressed forward.

We danced in the bedroom to a harmony of pleasure.

Each and every kiss, every touch we so treasured.

We shared a passionate adventure, sailing on the winds of intimacy.

This was magic, you and me, and it was so clear to see.

But then something inside you changed. Your thoughts suddenly shifted to the fears of shame.

I could feel your hands begin to tremble as you loosened your grip around me.

Your lips quivered and you opened up your eyes to see.

"I'm...sorry."

I told you there was nothing to apologize for.

"I'm not ready for this. Not ready for you and me."

I turned my head toward the bedroom door.

And as I listened for a moment to the autumn winds blowing outside the window that afternoon, I knew in my heart that this journey we had started was already doomed.

Fast forward one week. One week since I'd kissed you goodbye for the last time on the cheek.

"I'm sorry, but we just aren't compatible," you sent in a text.

It took me a while, but I finally realized you were just a broken mess.

"And I don't have any desire to talk to you or see you again."

At first I was confused, but now I'm glad it came to an end.

Because like the changing of seasons, it was time to let you fall like a dead leaf to the ground.

There are many seasons ahead. One day you'll come back to me and find that I'm happier than I've ever been, with all the love that I've found.

And with the leaves you'll blow away, far away into the distance. Eventually you'll crumble into fragments of resistance.

And the magic that lasted for just a minute will be lost forever in a sea of souls longing to be intimate.

Candy Land

This place is making us restless, but I think I've got a plan that just might leave you breathless.

Listen closely and I think you'll hear the sound of a train that's drawing very near.

It's soon to arrive, and I hope you'll join me. There's much for us to do, so much for our eyes to see.

So take my hand and let's blow this popsicle stand, and come see what I have planned.

All aboard, the train has arrived! I've got two golden tickets good for two hearts to be revived.

Time's a' wastin' and it's time to leave this station. To our destination- a permanent vacation!

The world will be our carousel. We'll spin round and round, without a care to be found.

We'll slide down into a world full of bliss, a place we'll call our own and never grow tired of, kiss after kiss.

We'll climb mountains of marshmallow fluff, slide down them on a giant cream puff.

We'll count clouds of cotton candy and swim in an ocean of your favorite brandy.

We'll swing from red licorice ropes and after that, we'll watch for UFOs from our rock candy telescopes.

The land will be sweet, but your kisses much sweeter. Who knows? Perhaps one day our sugar-coated adventures will be shown in a theater!

The rest of the world would be so jealous. "We too want to live in such a state of bliss," they'll tell us.

But this world is only made for you and me. A place filled with wonders as far as the eye can see.

Picture perfect, Part 1

She has convinced herself that she loves him because she doesn't feel like she deserves any better.

She's beautiful, he's handsome. In photographs they look perfect together.

The picture-perfect American family.

She tolerates his angry tantrums, endures the slaps, the hits, and holds her breath during the porn he forces her to watch with him.

She tries to distract herself with the kids when he goes out to the bar for hours on Friday nights.

But she chose him. He chose her. Till death do them part.

So when he takes his clothes off and pushes her against the wall, she knows she's no match for his physical strength. She knows she has no choice but to play along, play the role of the good little housewife, let him treat her like his personal plaything. And when he forces himself into her as he does so frequently, she forces a smile on her face and closes her eyes tightly, hoping it will somehow dissipate the unbearable pain.

She's still sore from last night. It feels like razor blades going in.

When he slams her down onto the bathroom floor and holds her down while he has his way with her, the only thought keeping her alive, keeping her from collapsing is her children, who are quietly sleeping in their bedrooms oblivious to the torturous scene.

She almost doesn't taste the blood from her busted lip as her face is smashed onto the tile floor, scraping the skin on her nose up and down, up and down.

She almost doesn't feel her bones cracking as he presses down on her back. Almost doesn't taste her salty tears on her lips.

For a moment their faces are all she can see. Their beautiful, peaceful faces. They look like angels. And just before their precious faces begin to smile back at her, reality hits her hard and suddenly the pain zips back and the vision fades.

He starts screaming and shouting, laughing as if he's deriving some kind of sick pleasure from what he's doing, but she can't hear his words. By the time she starts to feel something more than agonizing pain, she starts to black out.

When she wakes up it's the same as before. The same as every time before. Face down on the bathroom floor lying in splotches of her own blood, thankful she's alive, but terrified to live another day in this hell.

He's in the living room passed out on the couch after pleasuring himself to some porn that's still on the screen.

She slowly picks herself up and rises to her feet, nearly falling over from dizziness, hands clasping to the edge of the sink.

She doesn't dare look into the mirror to remind herself of what he's done to her.

Stumbling into the living room, she wipes the blood from her chin and quietly shuffles toward her twin daughters' bedroom door. Tears stream down her cheek as she rests her forehead on the door. She wants to weep so loudly, wants to scream at the top of her lungs. But she holds her tongue, because she doesn't want to wake them.

The pain below is unbearable, her body feels so weak as she collapses to the floor in front of the bedroom door. All she can do is lie there, wallowing in her fears, her anger, her depression while she waits for some grain of energy to return to her so she can get up before he wakes up.

Slowly the scene in front of her begins to fade to darkness. She can't keep her eyes open any longer. She wants so badly to fight it, but her body succumbs to exhaustion and she passes out on the floor.

This is her only respite. Her only escape from the pain.

Suddenly she feels something slam into her side as she comes back into consciousness.

As her eyes adjust she looks up and sees him standing above her, dressed from head to toe in his favorite three-piece suit.

If she didn't know any better she'd think he was a knight in shining armor, there to rescue her.

But that split second thought quickly disappears as she moves her leg and feels the pain again.

"What the hell are you doing? Get your ass up, bitch!"

"Wake the kids up and get them ready."

"It's time for church."

To be continued..

Inferno

Flame flickering, can you hear the bickering?

Wall on fire, picture frames smoldering.

What's that in your hand you're holding?

The phone clenched tightly in her hands;

The accusations of another man.

Screams and shouts across the room,

Each heated moment closer to their doom.

A vase filled with flowers he bought you flies across the room.

Crash! Tiny fragments scatter onto the floor.

There he goes, headed for the door.

A twist of the knob, but it doesn't turn.

Locked inside, they're bound to burn.

It was she who caused this.

It was he who caused this.

As the smoke billows, grab your tear-soaked pillows.

Hold your breath, this is going to be intense.

None of this is making any sense.

But it's too late now, no time to rewind.

You both had your chance to leave this all behind.

In this moment of weakness, when all is aflame,

Confusion sets in; who was really to blame?

Two former lovers cower on the floor,

A few more breaths before the end of this war.

A beam suddenly collapses and falls in between them.

"I'm so sorry, I love you Jim!"

The ring on his finger that he never took off,

Reminds him of what once was as he begins to cough.

His burned hand stretches toward her as he cries with his last breath,

"I'm so sorry, I love you too, Beth!"

A senseless war brought down with fire.

A lover's quarrel, a love that expired.

In the cold night air their bodies burn,

A story ends, now what lessons will be learned?

Don't ask me, I'm just the writer.

It's time to go - my pen is on fire.

The Heart

The curtain is drawn, and a passionate scene unfolds before us.

Two lovers embrace in the night. The moonlight's glow illuminates a canvas painted with what appears to be the perfect marriage of two soulmates.

Lovingly, they gaze into one another's eyes. Their hands embrace and they begin to dance for a moment before leaning in for a soft, passionate kiss. But the moonlight that night hides from the audience the important truth of the matter.

You can feel the passion in the air. The dancing so close, so harmonious. The lovers' souls melt into each other like a sweet symphony.

"I am yours forever, my love," he whispers in her ear.

But something isn't quite right.

Unbeknownst to him, she holds a dagger behind her back. The two lovers perpetually connect and lean in for kisses. And each time they embrace she stabs him in the heart. At first the dagger barely pierces the skin. But after a few stabs his chest starts to bleed and he puts his hand over the wound to stop the bleeding.

"It's ok, it's just a small wound, honey."

Again they try to embrace and she stabs him again in the heart. Blood pours everywhere.

"Honey, I love you. I...."

His shaking hands press against the gaping wound, but his fingers are futile in stopping the blood flow.

He stares into her beautiful eyes with confidence combined with bewilderment.

"It's ok, my dear. I...I still love you.."

The two embrace again, and she thrusts her dagger once more into his still beating, bleeding heart.

A look of dismay and confusion forms on his face as she stares emotionless at him. This time his heart begins to spill out of his chest onto the ground in a waterfall of blood.

He falls to his knees, and in a desperate attempt he scrambles to pick up his heart, but it keeps slipping through his fingers.

"Sweetheart, I've...got this...I swear...This heart...belongs to....you," he cries, choking on his own blood.

She remains silent.

"I Promise you...I'm going to make this work.." he nervously mumbles. "Just let me......pick this.....up.."

She kneels down before him, raises her dagger and stabs it into his heart over and over until it's broken into a thousand pieces in a pool of blood.

"This...can still..be saved...." he mumbles, falling over onto his face as he reaches one last time to grab what's left.

"I'm going to...put us back together, my dear. Just....give me....time."

She turns and walks away, not saying a word. And as she walks off into the night's void, he reaches his arm toward her and collapses.

The night fades to black.

Curtains close.

End scene.

Emptiness

It's like a ship without a sea, like a bird without a nest, like a desert without the sun.

The wind suddenly ceases to blow, disappearing into unknown places.

The crickets stop their evening symphony, the stars burn out and the night grows cold.

Purpose is ripped from our hands, Hope crashes to the ground into a million pieces.

Who will save us?

We ask, but no answer comes. We are on our own. Trapped on two opposite ends of this wall we've built, our knuckles bleeding from punching it over and over again. There's no way back to each other, no way over it.

Meaning ceases, darkness stretches as far as the eyes can see. The vast emptiness offers no comfort or hope.

Going back to each other is meaningless. So we've no choice but to press forward into the darkness. What's ahead? Who can say?

The only certainty is our graves. And when it's over, will we awake in a new world together?

Retrodead

I know you've found a love you don't regret, but so long ago you could have picked me instead.

When your head hits the soft pillow, do you ever dream of the places we would go?

When you're left alone with your thoughts as your only friend the days seem longer as you wait for the end.

Falling leaves remind me of the days we spent working at the old mill, stealing glances at one another like thieves.

We were young and innocent then, untainted by the wages of war and sin.

I tried to hide behind the mask of a wise man, hoping you wouldn't notice what I had planned.

It was that look in your eyes that saw through my clever disguise.

One glance and I was hooked, ready again to spark up a new romance.

I played it cool, trying not to seem like a fool, but you caught me dreaming of what we could be.

By some miracle, seemingly out of the blue, as it turned out you felt the same way too.

"In my mind's eye I can see it so clear, a beautiful future somewhere far away from here; a place devoid of you, a vast ocean filled with infinite shades of blue." — The Ghosts

Another American Dream

"Why don't you get off your fat ass and make dinner?"

There he goes again. The raised voice, the temper, the half-empty bottle of bud light. You just got home 20 minutes ago and took one minute for yourself. Just one minute to sit down and take a deep breath before heading back into the battle zone. He got home from his friend's house an hour before you, and he's already six bottles in.

You're exhausted. Today was a rough day at work. You coworkers tell you that at 8 months of pregnancy, you should just stay home and take it easy. But you don't want to stay at home because he'll be there all day. He lost his job four months ago, and you're the only one bringing money home, so what other choice do you have?

"What are you doing? I'm fucking hungry!"

You just want one moment to yourself. Just one.

His angry voice goes in one ear and out the other. Because you don't want to hear it. Not tonight.

You hear this every night, and you've told yourself a thousand times you'd leave him. You're tired of the way he treats you, tired of the abuse and sick of the pain he's caused you.

"Oh, but when he's sober he's not such a bad guy, really," you try to convince yourself.

But he was sober when he cheated on you with the neighbor across the street.

"Maybe someday he'll change. Maybe if he finds a more fulfilling job, he'll be happy, maybe when the baby is born he will become a better man and a good father."

But none of this will happen, and deep in your heart you know this.

He starts pacing the floor. This is your cue to get up before he starts throwing things. You'd just cleaned up the glass from the vase he threw at the wall last night. With the last bit of energy you have left to give, you pull yourself up from the couch.

"I promise someday things will be better," you whisper as you place your hand gently on your pregnant belly.

By the time dinner is ready, he'll be passed out on the couch. And when he wakes up at 11 p.m., he'll complain that the food is cold, as he usually does. But you slowly make your way into the kitchen anyway, because you still have to eat, and if you don't then the baby won't eat.

As you turn on the stove and move the spatula toward the meat, you get lost in your thoughts. As the meat begins to sizzle, you start day-dreaming of a life far away from here. Meeting a nice guy in a church somewhere who treats you right every day, never raises his voice at you, treats you with respect, and never touches a beer.

You smile for one brief moment, but then the smoke alarm goes off and sends you back to your cold reality.

You begin to panic.

"No! No, no, no. If he hears the smoke alarm he'll wake up and be upset!"

You grab a hand towel from the kitchen drawer and start fanning the smoke away.

The beeping stops. He's still passed out on the couch.

"Thank God."

You finish cooking dinner and sit down at the kitchen table alone, as usual.

What kind of life is this? How many times have you swore you'd break free, find some way to make things better?

Now you're pregnant with his baby, so you're stuck with him. Even if you left him, there would be a custody battle, he'd probably raise hell and then try to win you back, and if you didn't take him back, he'd do everything he could to make your life miserable.

Sometimes you wonder if there's any escape at all. Maybe you're stuck here. This is your lot in life. This is what you chose. Maybe God gave you one chance at love, and you blew it by "settling" for the wrong man.

Now it's too late to go back, no way to rewind the hands of time. This is your punishment, you figure. Maybe you deserve this. Maybe you just weren't meant to be happy.

All those times you've scrolled down the Facebook home page and watched the lives of your friends unfold in beautiful, filtered pictures of faraway coastal vacations, exciting birth announcements, and new homes purchased.

"They all look so happy. So perfect."

Why can't you have that? What did you do to deserve this?

You didn't ever plan on being with an abusive husband who drinks himself to sleep every night. He seemed so sweet in the beginning. Things were so wonderful the first year of being married.

But is anyone really ever happy? Do Facebook photos show the truth, or hide it?

As you take your last bite of the tuna casserole you made, somewhere across town, your best friend Jessica goes to bed alone, because her husband is out with his friends at a strip club.

Two states over, your friend Maria kisses her two year old goodnight. "Mommy loves you, and daddy loves you from heaven, too."

Your coworker Angelica is having painful sex with her boyfriend, who insists that they "make love," every night before going to bed, even though she's on her period.

Meanwhile Kelly, one of your bridesmaids at your wedding takes a handful of sleeping pills, hoping that she won't wake up the next day so she can escape the loneliness she feels while her husband sleeps peacefully beside her.

As you clean up your plate, you take one last glance at the couch. You can hear him snoring. You're exhausted, so you figure you'll just go to bed alone.

A tear streams down your cheek as you look down at your belly. You place your hand on it, and feel her kick.

Tonight is one of many to come that will be just like this one.

Tonight there is sadness on every block, regret looms around every corner, and hope seems all but choked out by the heavy fog of depression that lingers outside every bedroom window.

This is the American Dream. This is what you've always dreamed of. This is what every woman has dreamed of.

You think you're alone. That it's only you who has to suffer.

You don't realize it, but you're just another drop in an ocean of tears, another brick in the wall, another statistic.

And the American Dream will continue, as it has for decades.

I'll be your Jimmy Stewart and you'll be my Audrey Hepburn. The night will belong only to us.

I'll see you there soon. I'll be waiting... - The Ghosts

Was

I had a strange dream last night, of that there's no doubt.

I just can't seem to remember what it was all about.

I think you were there, or maybe you were not. I'll try to recall it, I'll give it a shot.

I thought we were together like we were so long ago. We were snuggling together during a late night picture show.

I put my arm around you and whispered that I loved you. You smiled at me and told me that you felt the same way too.

But suddenly an uneasy feeling came over me that for years I hadn't felt, and the movie reel upon the screen began to burst and melt.

The guilt and the shame caused by so many before, manifested itself in broken images on the screen like some sort of twisted encore.

"What's wrong honey?" You asked me with fright, while the demons of my past began to dance with delight.

"You'll never be happy, of that we are sure."

"We've watched you fail miserably so many times before."

Everything inside me told me to run. But no matter how hard I tried, I couldn't budge an inch, not even one. Kept looking for an exit door, but couldn't even see one.

And slowly the walls began to close in on me. This was my gruesome fate, it was very plain to see.

But then I woke up, and saw you lying next to me.

Even after all this time, I wonder why I'm still filled with worry.

Maybe it's because you're a dream come true.

A dream that I want to live out every single day with no one else but you.

Innocence Lost

Warm summer night, 1962. 11 p.m.

They're cruising down the highway in a blue 1957 Plymouth.

"Sherry," by Frankie Valli comes onto the radio.

"Hey, this song is hot! Crank it up, Jimmy!" Susan shouts, before taking another drink.

"Sherry, can you come out tonight? To my twist party (come out) where the bright moon shines (come out), we'll dance the night away!"

They start singing along at the top of their lungs.

There are four of them. They're headed to Jimmy's house for an after-prom party.

Jimmy, Susan, Tom and Madison. All dressed up in their dapper tuxedos and cute dresses.

So young and beautiful, so full of youthful enthusiasm and naivety.

Cool October night, 2014. 11 p.m. James and Teresa are in a boat on Lake Eufaula. They've just finished making love, and as Teresa buttons up her shirt, a cold chill suddenly comes over her.

"James! Can we...can we go back now?"

"What's wrong, honey? Don't you wanna go another round?" James says slyly.

"No. And that's not funny. This was a bad idea."

Jimmy is getting more smashed by the minute. His vision begins to blur. The car swerves to the left and crosses the center line before he corrects himself.

Madison, the only uncomfortable, sober one in the car adjusts her cat eye glasses and takes a deep breath. She has finally had enough, and breaks her silence.

"Jimmy, this isn't funny! Slow the hell down!" She shouts.

James and Teresa begin their short journey back to shore. The only light they have is the glow of the full moon above.

"You're such a scaredy cat, Teresa."

"What am I supposed to feel? Pure joy? This whole idea was creepy to begin with! I mean, who does this, anyway? This boat is dirty. I swear if I get a rash.."

Suddenly the boat shakes for a moment.

"What the hell was that!"

Time slows to a crawl on this warm summer night as the Plymouth careens off the edge of the road and drops twenty feet into the lake below.

A skeletal hand rises up from the watery depths, barely visible by the moonlight's glow. Its bony fingers silently clasp the edge of the boat.

"Did you hear something, James?"

The boat begins to shake back and forth steadily.

Teresa screams.

"What the..." James murmurs as he swings his head behind him to look into the water.

The boat suddenly stops shaking.

Teresa feels the bony grip of the decayed wet hand clasp tightly around her left leg. She screams in terror.

The car quickly fills up with water as it begins to sink into the lake. Jimmy tries desperately to open the driver's side door, but to no avail. In the back seat the water rises quickly, as Susan and Madison gasp for air, arms flailing uncontrollably as the pearl necklace that Madison borrowed from her mother floats to the ceiling of the back seat. Within moments they've taken their last breaths before slowly and agonizingly succumbing to their watery grave.

In the front seat, Jimmy and Tom try desperately to free themselves as the car steadily sinks to the lake's bottom. Tom manages to get his door open, and begins to squeeze out the narrow opening, but as the car hits the bottom, the door closes on his chest, knocking what little breath he had left out of his water-filled lungs.

It's hopeless. On this fateful night these four teens met their end at the bottom of Lake Eufaula.

Their bodies were never found.

Theresa is yanked violently into the lake as James desperately tries to hang onto her. Her shrill screams echo out into the night, but there isn't a soul around within earshot who can save them.

The next day, the small aluminum fishing boat James and Theresa were in was found turned upside down on the shore by a fisherman. When authorities arrived and examined the boat, James' mangled corpse was found lying underneath it. A few feet up the shore was the detached leg of Theresa, rotting in the afternoon sun.

Leftover entrails from their bodies created a trail to the water's edge, where a detached bony hand clasping a pearl necklace had washed ashore.

The rotting skeletal remains of all four teens were found resting inside the rusted 1957 Plymouth lying at the bottom of Lake Eufaula on October 15, 2014.

After 52 years spent rotting below, the four missing teens had finally found rest.

James and Theresa however, weren't so lucky.

Companion

A lifetime ago your tiny arms held me so tightly. Each night you'd whisper into my ear that you loved me. Through thunderstorms and sleepless nights, I was there for you and kept you safe.

Under the covers we shared so much laughter. My stuffing soaked up so many tears, my nose felt your warm kisses every night before your mother turned off your bedroom lights.

You held me tightly and said you'd never let go.

Fast forward. Years have passed, and I'm sitting on a lonely shelf in an antique shop. You've long passed on. You grew up, forgot about me, found love, had two beautiful children. You waved goodbye to them as they left for college. You held your husband's hand tightly as he took his last breath. Your frail body withered away and even as you spoke your last words, I still hadn't forgotten about you. The little girl who loved me, who wrapped her tiny arms around me each night, who whispered all her hopes and dreams and fears into my ear. Who loved me unconditionally through every smile and every tear.

I miss you and the love you once gave me. I miss each kiss and each giggle, each thunderclap we braved together, each argument your parents had that we carefully listened to.

So now I sit here, lonely but hopeful, that one day I'll find a home again with a special someone who will hold my brittle stuffed body in their arms and love me like you did so many decades before.

Inside me these silent memories of you will never fade. And whoever holds me next will never know what we shared so long ago. But I won't ever forget, and your legacy will live on in these fragile strands.

"Like a hollow ghost, she sits in front of her vanity every night alone" - The Ghosts

Porcelain

"I never want to let you go," she spoke softly into my ear.

"I feel so safe in your arms," she whispered.

I looked into her eyes and smiled. "I'll always protect you."

I held her in my arms so tightly that night. As we shared those moments of bliss, I never wanted it to end.

But suddenly I could feel her fragile limbs begin to crack between my fingers.

"What's wrong?" I asked her.

"I'm sorry," she whispered, looking into my eyes with the saddest, most helpless gaze.

"Was I holding you too tightly, my dear?" I asked.

I tried to maintain my composure, but I could feel her fragile body collapsing in my arms.

Then as I put my hand on the back of her head, it began to crumble away.

With one final somber gaze, her face began to crack away and disintegrate before me.

Pieces of her began to fall, bouncing off my chest and legs before crashing to the ground.

As the dust settled I began to cough. I stood there utterly mystified as to what had just happened.

I kneeled down as my tears soaked the porcelain fragments lying on the ground and immediately tried to gather the pieces and put them back together in a panic.

But it was useless. She was gone.

And for the rest of my life I was plagued with questions without answers.

Hollow questions, filled with emptiness, like porcelain.

The Silver Strand

On a dusty shelf, tucked away in an old library rests her final read, a worn red book that's been resting for decades.

Neglected for so long, yet its pages still hide a piece of her inside among black letters that once danced for her brown eyes.

A silver strand, once flowing like a beautiful river from her scalp, rests between pages 34 and 35.

She's been gone for 42 years now, resting beneath green weeds crawling their way over her granite tombstone.

Such a beautiful shade of brunette, that strand of hair once radiated when she'd walk into a room and run her fingers through it.

That beautiful pearl smile held such allure for those who were lucky enough to witness the joy she brought with her wherever she went.

The first thing she noticed when her eyes met him was the olive suit he was wearing. It was her least favorite color, but his eyes more than made up for it. She'd never seen such a beautiful shade of green in the sparkle of his warm gaze.

So blue was the ocean on that first date, as they sat on a red and white checkered blanket spreading yellow mustard on turkey sandwiches as the wind threatened to carry it away to the seagulls.

Never had he seen such beauty wrapped in white the day they said "I do."

When she saw him step onto the stage wearing a black tuxedo with that red boutonniere, try as she may, she couldn't fight back her tears of joy when he smiled at her.

Her first glimpse of her daughter's olive complexion as she exited her mother's womb provided instant relief and unspeakable joy to her excited, rapidly beating heart.

The sky was always a stunning shade of orange as she'd watch the sunset with him on their back porch every evening as they'd share a glass of dark red wine.

There were so many colors in those black and white days.

So many memories remain in that silver strand hidden away from the modern world, so much beauty and a love that's never-ending.

Such a radiant red was the final rose you received from him before you stood before heaven's door.

Such a beautiful shade of blue was the sky that final day, not a single tear from Heaven was shed.

They say that when one goes away, if the skies are not gray, God is ready and waiting to embrace their souls into the radiant glow of eternal bliss.

You may be gone, but these pages haven't forgotten. One day this silver strand will shine again, as radiant as the woman who carried it with her so many decades ago.

History Ablaze

Today some take for granted the beautiful shade of their skin. But not so long ago, such beauty was considered a sin.

In the city of Tulsa, back in the black and white days, an important part of history was set ablaze.

A dark stain on American society, a clash of colors was fought in streets that caused near-forgotten notoriety.

Blood was shed, people were killed. It would take decades for the scars to be healed.

And yet much of what happened was eventually kept quiet. But now the world must know the truth of the Tulsa race riots.

A young white woman's scream on Memorial Day weekend, a young black man a prosperous community would soon try to defend.

White or black, who was really to blame? On the outside different shades, but inside all the same.

Hundreds were slain, their bodies tossed into pits as if to flush them down the drain.

But these were human beings, with hopes and dreams and fears. So why have they disappeared and become forgotten for all these years?

While pedestrians pass by on their morning routine, six feet underground their bodies rest, waiting for the day when again they shall be seen.

Unsung heroes of yesteryear, so many stories untold because they are no longer here.

Covered in soil, these brave men and women, yesterday warriors who fought.

They fought for the right to live, the right to breathe, the right to simply exist.

But in this world, the dark color of your skin was, and still is, a reason to be dismissed.

Against the odds, they built a thriving community, a booming district, Black Wall Street was beaming with pride.

And yet their success was fueling contemptuous hate from the outside.

On a hot summer night, the spiteful mob arrived with their torches, green with envy.

"But the blacks have more than me!"

Was it worth killing a fellow man because of jealousy?

What followed was the worst race riot in the history of the city.

It was a crime of racism, covered up by lies and cynicism.

Their families were murdered, engulfed in flame, their homes were ravaged.

Acts of unspeakable cruelty committed by the "superior" savages.

Did entire city blocks have to burn, so such a lesson to be learned?

No human life was worth taking for this. Whether black or white, all of us have sinned. No need to point fingers, but that's what put them in the hell they were in.

It wasn't their choice to be despised. They'd done nothing wrong, committed no sin.

But they were the target of hate, simply for their dark melanin.

For decades their stories would be silent, meant to be forgotten.

Their witnesses stifled, their families chased away like vermin.

But history cannot be erased, despite what their murderers intended.

Their stories will come to light through our voices, until racism is ended.

Dedicated to the victims of the Tulsa Race Riots of 1921.

"Silence speaks louder than words, the worst thing I've never heard." — The Ghosts

Chapters

If I could capture the moon in a jar for you, would you use it as a night light beside your bed?

If I wrote a novel for you, would it ever truly get read?

What can I do for you that would make you happy?

Do you really mean it when you say that you want nothing more in this world than me?

Will you write new chapters of this life with me?

Will we make beautiful stories together that we may one day take off the shelf to fondly reminisce?

Together we'll be the hand that writes, our love for one another the pen. Our blood will be the ink that touches the pages with the beauty of countless blissful memories.

Let's fill these bookshelves with bestsellers, paperback romances and adventures to places only we can go.

Liberty?

The whole world felt his pain when the bullet entered his brain: another black man slain.

The tremors beneath your feet aren't a load of crock; the earth trembles when another innocent is shot.

Life is more than just a race, and in case you haven't heard there's no wine waiting for you at the finish line.

Who gave you the right to point fingers at daydreamers and truth singers fighting for better days under this racist haze when you should be ashamed of the color your skin represents and the history of sin carried with it by hateful men?

You better humble yourself before you fall, before your own blood is spilled in sacred halls, before more words of hate are scrawled out on whitewashed walls.

Stop entertaining the dark thoughts in your brain and start seeing that your actions are doing nothing to take away the pain.

Maybe you're too afraid to admit that you're insane , admit you find comfort in knowing that our hearts beat the same.

Maybe it's not crazy to think that we all beat as one drum, that without working together the world would be numb.

We're tired of all the lies, so say your goodbyes to self and listen to the wise.

The color of our skin is not the sin.

The sin is holding in the love God gave you and locking it up so tightly within.

Don't let the past dictate who are today, don't let generations of prejudice convince you that this is the American way.

Est Finis

So many years adrift at sea, never knew you were waiting for me.

I could feel you in my beating heart; so

many times it would start and stop.

Floating aimlessly with no direction, trying to picture you in the moon-light's projection.

Into the night air I called out to you with what little air my lungs could carry.

With each wave of silence my hope would be buried.

But not forever, as I thought it would seem.

Because all along you were out there, my future queen.

So now that we've found this shore, let's walk forward together and see what else is in store.

"Our love is eternal, our passion infinite.
Neither time nor space will ever stop us.

We just have to find each other
first." – The Ghosts

Inadequate

My mind is cloudy but I'll never quit.

I can still hear them whispering:

"Inadequate."

Subliminal messages conquer my thoughts as I sink further into this miserable pit.

"Inadequate."

I'll find my way out, one step at a time as I take hit after painful hit.

"Inadequate."

You think you've trapped me? Think again. I'm coming for you, you miserable piece of shit.

"Inadequate."

Stop telling me that I can't do this, quit holding me back when I'm trying to stand. I refuse to give in, I refuse to sit.

"Inadequate."

I'm like a square peg in a circle-shaped hole, aren't I? No matter how hard I try I'll never quite fit.

"Inadequate."

I'm tired of being scorned, tired of being ripped apart bit by bit.

"Inadequate."

I really can't do this, can I? This really is the end of all things. This is really it, isn't it?

"Inadequate."

I guess I'm not the woman I thought I was, as hard as it is to admit.

"Inadequate."

My time is up, the end has come. 27 years and I guess I'll never get it.

"Inadequate."

There's no going back now, it's too late. I've accepted my fate, these wrists are slit.

"Inadequate."

"She has convinced herself that she loves him because she doesn't feel like she deserves any better." — The Ghosts

Jack

On an abandoned farm in the Oklahoma countryside, there is an old stone next to a rusted barbed wire fence. On that stone, there is a name etched into it: "Rusty" That is all it says.

Now, you wouldn't know it today, judging by the overgrowth of weeds and twisted trees, but some time ago, many moons ago, this farm was full of life. And there was none livelier on the homestead than a little boy named Jack. Let's explore the story of little Jack, shall we?

The year was 1920. Jack had just turned six years old when his father gave him a very special gift for his birthday: a beautiful black and white Boston Terrier puppy whom he named Rusty.

It didn't take long for Jack and Rusty to be attached at the hip. Every Saturday, Jack would hunt for the perfect walking stick, and they'd stroll along the forest surrounding the farm looking for adventure.

"Rusty! Look out! There's a dragon over there!" Jack would shout out

Rusty would play along as if they were slaying the fiery beast, barking and growling followed by some playful lunging. The pair loved their adventures, and would spend hours exploring their home. They saw it with fresh eyes each morning as if it were a new place. They had so much fun they stayed outside most days until Jack's mother called them in for supper.

"C'mon boy! I think I can smell the pork chops and fresh biscuits from here! I think we've earned ourselves a feast today!" Jack would call to Rusty as they rushed back home. At the end of each day, they would fall into bed next to each other and be fast asleep in the blink of an eye.

Nothing beats the love between a boy and his dog.

The Summer of 1920 however, would be their only summer together.

On the morning of July 17th, Jack woke up to realize he couldn't move his legs. Try as though he might, they just wouldn't budge.

"Mom! Mom!!" He screamed out.

Jack's mother ran into his bedroom to find her son in tears, screaming.

"I can't feel them, mom! I can't feel my legs!!"

Days passed and Jack's mom tended to the boy tirelessly day and night. He had been complaining of a sore throat for a few days before the 17th, but suddenly that sore throat spiraled into more serious symptoms. Poor Jack couldn't even walk himself to the bathroom. His mother cared for him through his spiking fever, refusal to drink water, and his slow paralysis.

Rusty also never left Jack's side. He gave his best friend's fingers a lick as if that might make the boy feel better. As Jack grew weaker, and each breath more labored, Rusty never budged.

"It's not over, boy. We've got lots of adventures ahead, I promise!"

Rusty buried his face under Jack's arm as the boy took his last breath. Shortly after, the poor dog too, took his last without a complaint.

September 28, 2020. There was a new owner of the house named Kevin. He had been hearing some weird things so he decided to keep a journal.

"I heard footsteps again last night. It must have been around 3:30 a.m.

I couldn't go back to sleep so I took some NyQuil." This was the first entry found.

October 1, 2020.
"I heard what sounded like a child screaming while I was doing laundry today. There were no kids outside. It's the middle of nowhere, for Pete's sake."

October 5, 2020.
"My god, I saw him. A little boy dressed in overalls standing in the doorway of the spare bedroom. His face was pale and his eyes were black. I stood there in horror staring at him for what seemed like forever, and as I backed away he vanished."

October 14, 2020.
"So help me God, I don't know what the hell this thing is or what its purpose is. I've seen the boy four times now, and he seems harmless, but something doesn't sit right with me. I heard a dog barking last night. I don't own a dog and there are no neighbors around for miles."

October 16, 2020.
"I woke up with a damn bite mark on my arm! A freaking bite mark! Looks like some kind of animal got me. How is this even possible? What the hell is going on? I don't feel so good."

October 17, 2020.

"That's so weird that I'm not going to make it. Isn't it weird? Isn't this a good dream? Isn't this it, boy?"

October 20, 2020.
"Dogs are awesome too awesome thank goodness I don't have any more friends than I ever had to go through I was a kid that I had no fun with that night and that's it all the way to the world so that's what kind words you have imagined and you have no fun and and and and and and and and everything is going to be ok perfect perfect perfect perrr....."

Kevin was found lying in a pool of his own blood five days later. There were bloody dog prints leading outside through the front door. Investigators ruled his death to be caused by rabies, but they could never find the source.

"Do your worst, because I'm ready to do my best." – The Ghosts

Lost and Gone Forever

Find me before what's left of me is gone.

Before these shadows close in on me.

Save me before there's nothing left worth saving.

The waves are coming in, and soon my innocence will drift away into the ocean.

The vultures overhead are circling, waiting to peck away at the last bit of sanity left inside my mind.

I'm weakened from this fast-paced life, tired of running this rat race to which there is no finish line.

I can't wait much longer.

I was told you'd be here, but all I see is this empty beach stretching across the horizon.

Like a hypocrite who doubts their religion, I'm losing faith in you, losing faith in myself.

If you're out there, then come to me.

Find me before what's left of me fades away forever.

Splat

January 28, 1986:

"Desperate people do crazy things."

The final words spoken by Cynthia before she pulled the trigger that fateful morning.

All it took was one bullet to rip through Gary's skull and penetrate his brain, ending his life with a spray of blood that saturated her sleeve.

It was a night of revelry, filled with liquor and lines of cocaine - typical for the two of them on a weeknight.

Lovers and addicts are all the same. Whether the addiction is a chemical substance or endorphins saturating the brain.

It was jealousy that drove her to pick up the nine millimeter.

Gary's blood flowed like a river onto the linoleum floor. Their cat Muffy, as if completely oblivious to what had happened, stuck her nose down to the blood and took a few sniffs before deciding this substance wasn't something she was interested in tasting.

Before the smell of sulfur had dissipated, Cynthia had already disappeared.

She'd hastily driven away from the scene of the crime, hoping she could get out of town before the cops found out.

As she turned onto the highway, a large spat hit her windshield. It was a mosquito that was filled with human blood.

"Shit! What the hell?"

Cynthia frantically tried using her windshield wipers to scrape it away, but the wipers wouldn't turn.

"You've got to be kidding me!"

Wednesday, 8:30 p.m. Two days before the murder. Gary and Cynthia had finished a big fight in the kitchen over a love note she'd received from another man. Tired of listening to her excuses, Gary decided to grab the dog leash hanging from a hook on the wall.

"I'm taking Muffin for a walk."

"Good," Cynthia murmured. "I hope you don't fucking come back either!"

Walking the dog was a respite from Gary's painful reality with Cynthia. Sure, neither of them were even close to being functional together, but at the end of the day, they knew they couldn't live without each other.

A small mosquito lands on Gary's neck and in a fraction of a second pokes its proboscis into his neck, sucking in a rich drink of his blood.

"Son of a.."

Gary slaps his neck, thinking he's killed it, but the mosquito escapes unscathed with a belly full of crimson sustenance.

Cynthia's trembling hands grasp the steering wheel as she continues down the highway, the blood stain still obscuring her view. She can't stop now. If she did, the cops might see her. They could be on her trail right now.

She couldn't get that blood splatter out of her mind. It was right in front of her, reminding her of what she'd done. Like a bad curse, it stayed with her during the two hour drive south into Sedona.

Finally, she found a secluded hotel in the middle of nowhere and decided to rest.

Thursday, 24 hours before the murder. She wants to leave him. She feels stuck, living in the same house with what feels like a complete stranger. He makes a little money, but just barely enough to get by. He pays for her drugs, which is really the only reason she's still around. She knows about his "secret stash" he keeps on a shelf in the closet. Last time she checked, it was filled with hundred dollar bills, mostly from drug sales.

Cynthia sat in her lonely hotel room, flipping through the wad of cash, closing her eyes as the flipping of the paper sings its rigid tune.

Was it worth it? Did she really have to kill him to get that money? She wouldn't have much time to think.

Suddenly a loud crash occurs outside her window. She looks outside and sees two men breaking into her van.

"Hey! What the hell do you think you're doing?!" She screams at them as she runs out the door in her bathrobe, lit cigarette dangling from her dry lips.

The windshield had been busted into pieces. Glass was strewn all over the sidewalk in front of her hotel room.

"Ouch! Mother fu.."

Cynthia realized she was barefoot. She looked down and saw a piece of glass stuck in her big toe. It was gushing blood.

One year ago. Dr. Hoffman's office.

"Listen, uh...you're not going to tell anyone about this? Right? I mean... my wife, she can't find out."

Gary nervously rubbed his hands together.

"It's ok, Gary. As your doctor I'm not obligated to tell anyone unless it's at your personal discretion."

It was HIV. Probably from a dirty needle. He wouldn't tell Cynthia. He figured he would ride it out and she'd be none the wiser.

"Rock Hudson has done just fine, right doc? This ain't nothing. Life goes on, right?"

It's not like he'd transfer it to her. He and Cynthia hadn't had sex in over two years.

Cynthia yanked out the shard of glass and fell to the ground. It was the worst pain she'd ever felt.

"Holy mother of.."

As she screamed in agony, when her teary eyes cleared for a moment, she realized the piece of glass she pulled out that she was still holding was already stained with blood.

"That damn mosquito! Fucking karma!"

But Cynthia was already doomed. She just didn't realize it yet.

The vandals were already long gone. The van was next to useless now, and she couldn't report it for fear of the police finding her.

As she dragged herself to the motel door, she could hear a buzzing sound from somewhere in the distance.

And that's when it happened.

The next morning, Cynthia's mutilated body was found lying flattened in the parking lot of the motel. Authorities claimed that a massive object had fallen on her from a great height.

At 11:38 a.m. that day, the Challenger space shuttle exploded 73 seconds into flight, killing the lives of all on board. Debris from the shuttle was scattered for miles around the surrounding area.

Cynthia was in the wrong place at the wrong time. Was this mere coincidence, or something more? Divine retribution?

Some secrets aren't meant to be revealed, some mysteries never meant to be solved.

"Half a lifetime to find you is quite the bargain for an eternity to spend with you in Eden's garden." — The Ghosts

Circus Maximus

It's a circus out there. Thoughts go back and forth like swinging trapeze artists. Ideas as sporadic as the sticky kettle corn that litters an arena. Everyone is cheering and clapping at the wonders of the modern age from their perception, but no one bothers to take a look at the ugly truths. Not even when they barge in like a raging bull, and are as large as an elephant in a small room.

If you want to make strides in life, you have to dress the part. It's all about looking nice.

If you want to find love, it's totally easy. You simply have to change everything about your very being. Become the enemy you've sworn never to be. Murder the old you and start fresh, because just as you are is not good enough for the new standards of today's age.

The gentlemen have been slaughtered to make way for new assholes. Good men have been replaced by self-centered narcissists and spoiled brats that have yet to stop suckling from their mother's breasts.

Quick, sprinkle some sugar and spread the veil to cover the ugly darkness. No one wants to see such horrid sights. No one wants to hear such blasphemy!
These are wholesome times. These are family-friendly days filled with strong morals and old-fashioned values. How dare we speak of the evils of this world? How dare we let our minds become corrupted by reality? Who needs truth? These comfy clouds fit the shape of our frowning faces quite nicely, don't you think?

What is truth, anyway? What is reality in these days of uncertainty?

Let's toss the shit of the world onto a blank canvas, spread it around blindly, and see what picture we can paint with the refuse today. "It's so bright and beautiful!" the world exclaims. The sad reality is the colors of truth are a dull and lifeless black and gray.

Can you hear that? A man is groaning in agony in the distance. His chest rattles as he prepares to take his final breath. That's the sound of a man who's given up, a lost soul out of time. He is out of dignity. He is out of hope. It's another portrait that is covered by the tapestry or the "American Dream". Another innocent life drowning in the ocean of failure.

Spread my cold, naked body out for all the world to see.
Crucify me before the hungry onlookers and ravenous souls that are simply starving for affection. One by one they will walk by, examining me inch by inch in the hunt for satisfaction.

Swipe this cross to the right if you're interested. Swipe it left if you'd rather gaze at another man's baking flesh.
Is my forced smile cheerful enough for you to feel better about your-self? Are my eyes the right shade of green?
Is my beard the perfect length?
Is my dick big enough for you? Will it fit into that empty space between your legs just right? Are my arms strong enough to carry you through the rising waves of your daddy drama? Are my abs the right shape for you to rest your cold hands upon while we're sleeping?

"Always judge a book by its cover."
Isn't that what your parents taught you?

Take a good look at me. Pick me to pieces. Tear me apart limb from limb as you open up my chest. Poke and prod my gentle heart until it bleeds.

Watch me suffer, spit out blood and scream in agony with what little breath my lungs have left. Watch as I writhe in pain as you apathetically pull out your lipstick and apply another coat.

"He's pretty average looking, but he might be good enough in bed."

How many good fucks do you think I'm worth? How many wild flings of passion do you have left in you before your body grows tired of physical pleasure and you can't perform on the playground anymore?

If sex is currency, you're a millionaire. You're swimming in the slippery capital as if it will never grow old. But how long until you're broke? Dried up like a bank account during the 1920's? We all run out of stamina sometime and where will you be then? Still next to me or in the arms of some CrossFit wannabe?

I'm just another dime a dozen in your eyes. A quick screw to waste your time. If my phallic member doesn't fill the empty void between your thighs, you can just keep flashing those perky little tits till you find "Mr. Right". Keep scrolling the mindless hookup sites looking for the perfect fit. It's worked this long, hasn't it?

How many seeds have you tainted with your insatiable lust? How many screaming children have exited your womb never knowing their fathers and never feeling the genuine love of a mother who cares?

How many tiny brains have been pierced by the sharp point of a coat hanger to satisfy selfish desires? How much innocent blood has been washed down the drain on drunken nights to eschew responsibility for the living?

I'd rather die than become another statistic. If this is it, I give up. I'd rather fade from existence than be lost in a digital hell where all the "undesired" end up.

It's an ugly thing, this masquerade we play. We hide behind fragile false facades. We paint beautiful pictures of our lives on digital landscapes for the world to worship. It all ends the same. Smiling in photos as we smear our children, friends and loved ones through the ink for our own personal gain.

They're only casualties of our own sick version of reality. Bystanders that we present to satisfy our own selfish desires. How many filters does it take to make you look beautiful? How much makeup will you need to apply to finally find yourself in bed with a man who will leave you feeling empty night after night?

Your selfish nature has caused you to paint yourself as the center of your own reality. Your greed makes you take without the thought of giving back. You're bitter and you hate when you don't feel loved. You ghost your latest entertainment when you've grown bored of their caring natures.

Our bodies have grown but our minds still crawl.
The bottle is empty but we never stopped sucking. The diapers are gone but we've never stopped shitting on one another.

Life is a playpen filled with toys. Human hearts we play tug of war with every day. When the time comes and we don't get what we want we scream, we cry and throw tantrums to try to change the outcome.
Social media is our nursery. Commenters are our caregivers. We live on a formula filled with likes and loves. We'll suck and suck until the accolades run dry.
Then what?

A meaningless period of living carved out of mountains built from our selfish desires for attention. We are nothing but toddlers who crave a perfect existence.

Are you still human without your digital connection? Are you still alive if your virtual heart stops beating? Maybe it's time to pull the plug. End the suffering in this electronic plane.

Oh, but suicide is something we won't mention here.
How dare we?

Life is filled with happiness, with plenty of funny cat videos and silly TikToks. There are endless streams of memes to keep us smiling, and plenty of weed to keep us high to numb the pain as we drown in oceans of alcohol bottled in so many beautiful colors to chase our sorrows with.

That's what life is all about isn't it?
Sex, drugs and rock n' roll, the whole shebang. We may have evolved from the days of the past, but we have certainly never changed. We pretend to have control, but we can't even seem to see the road. We will be fine if we just pray to our judgmental pastor and plaster on a smile. It will be okay. We never lost control anyway. Just put on a smile, turn the TV on and watch our daily soaps.

The young and restless present a future filled with hope, equality and peace. But as I observe the world, that's not what I see. Every day I'm watching the fall of Rome play out as I stare at my phone screen, but I have no idea what to do. I'm watching a societal collapse that everyone seems blind to.

The circus will continue, as it always has. So come one, come all to bear witness to the greatest show on earth - the planet's final gasp of air before the curtains close.

Rain

As the rain quietly trickles down, I wonder what you're thinking tonight.

Is it lonely where you are? Do you sometimes reach out your arm only to find an empty space where the love you've always sought should be? Do you ever wake up from dreams of what could be and wonder when such fantasies will become reality?

Your body may feel comfortable between the warm sheets, but is your soul? Is there a void there that you desire to fill in some way?

Listen to the rhythm of the falling rain. Can you hear my voice in the soft pattering of the percussive droplets? Can you hear my soft voice whispering that everything is going to be ok?

Some say the worst is yet to come, but I say the best is just over the horizon for future lovers like you and I.

Hold on to your pillow tightly as you grasp onto those happy thoughts that keep you going each day. Get lost in the steady rhythm of your dreams, sink down into waves of passion and let your soul float freely on the sweet thoughts I'm sending your way tonight.

Let's meet in our dreams. I'll build you a castle and I'll be waiting for you at the top of it. I'll save a special dance for you and I, and we will spin on the clouds together to the melody of songs once played on old silver screens.

I'll be your Jimmy Stewart and you'll be my Audrey Hepburn. The night will belong only to us.

I'll see you there soon. I'll be waiting…

"Sometimes the answers you seek are in the fabric of days gone by. Focus, and you'll see a clear picture unfold before your very eyes." — The Ghosts

Illusion

"I'm sorry, but your princess is in another castle."

I was five years old. It was a Saturday morning. 8 a.m. I slowly rolled out of my bed and stood up before giving myself a good stretch and a yawn, then wiped the morning sand from my eyes. I grabbed my favorite teddy bear and began my descent down the stairs, as I did every morning. My routine was simple. I'd walk into the kitchen, where my mom would greet me with a "Good morning, sleepyhead!" and have a bowl of cereal ready for me and a tall glass of orange juice. Life was great. All sunshine and happy memories. But there was one part of my life that made life a little brighter. Her name was Devon. She was the little girl who lived across the street, and she was my best friend and my first crush.

Every summer morning, I'd eat breakfast as fast as possible, so I could get dressed and ready for Devon to arrive at my front door to play. She was always the highlight of every day for me. We'd held hands, kissed each other on the cheek a few times, but mostly we had fun throwing sand in each other's hair and making mud pies in the backyard.

As I continued down the stairs, I wiped my eyes one more time and as my vision became clearer I could see my mom standing at the bottom of the stairs with tears in her eyes.

"Honey? I...have something to tell you."

She looked at me with a forced smile on her face, as if that would some-how help the bad news she was about to deliver.

"Honey, Devon and her family, well....they moved away last night."

What? What did she mean "moved away?" And why didn't I know anything about this?

"I'm sorry. I wanted to tell you last night, but I didn't want you to go to bed upset."

Mom was doing what any good parent would do. She did what she thought was best to protect her son's feelings.

"No."

"No. That's not true, mom. You're lying!" I shouted.

I suddenly raced through the living room and stormed out the front door before my mom had time to think.

"Honey, wait!"

By the time I hit the front porch steps my eyes were filled with tears and I couldn't see straight.

"No! This can't be true! I know she's still there!" I thought, as I crossed the street to her house, not even taking a moment to observe the traffic situation.

I climbed up the steps leading to her front door, still in my pajamas and started pounding on the door with my fists.

"Devon! Devon! I know you're there! Please answer!" I shouted over and over again, until finally I collapsed onto the porch, weeping.

My best friend was gone. My summer was over. And as far as I was concerned, my entire life was over at five years old.

"No, this can't be true. This isn't real. Why would this happen?"

My sadness turned to anger.

"Why would you do this, Devon?!" I screamed as I slammed my fist down.

I sat there with my head between my legs for what seemed like an eternity, when I felt the gentle touch of my mother's hand on my shoulder.

"I'm sorry. We wanted to tell you, but we didn't know how to break the news to you."

She held me in her arms until I finally stopped crying. After she explained everything, I still wasn't happy about it.

Life went on as it does, and soon the five year old me was kissing girls on the cheek behind bushes during recess, passing love notes in class and trying not to get caught, and going on many first dates.

As the years passed, sometimes I'd stop and wonder what ever happened to Devon. The internet was in its early days, and finding someone online wasn't as easy as it is today. So I never really had any way of knowing what happened to her.

Yet, in some sort of hopeless romantic kind of way, in the back of my mind I always wondered if one day we'd be reunited somehow, and we'd magically fall in love and realize we were destined to be together.

Girls came and went, the teenage years came and heartbreaks were aplenty, but somehow I survived. I'd lived the teenage dream and had my fair share of romance by the time college rolled around. In October 2006, I'd just ended a particularly taxing relationship, and I was ready to live the single life for a while. Between classes and journalism projects (with the occasional late night video game sessions) I stayed pretty busy, and that's exactly the way I wanted it.

But then destiny, or whatever you'd like to call it, came calling.

One night I was sitting at my computer playing a game, when suddenly Devon entered my mind. There was no particular reason for this, and I hadn't thought of her in what seemed like years.

"Hmm. I wonder what ever happened to her," I thought.

And then came the inkling to check my email.

So I did.

And when I saw the message from Devon in my inbox, I nearly passed out.

It's true. There in my inbox was a message from none other than Devon herself. It read something like, "Hey Corey! I don't know if you remember me or not, but I'm Devon, the girl you used to play with when we were kids! How have you been? If you'd like to chat some time, here's my phone number. I'd love to hear from you!"

I couldn't believe it. This was it, wasn't it? That glorious reunion I'd hoped for all those years. I'd give her that call, we'd hit it off and the next thing I knew, we'd be walking down the aisle together. That's how storybook romances work, right?

That night I picked up my phone and nervously dialed her number.

Ring.

Ring.

Ring.

"Ok, maybe she won't pick up. Maybe this is a stupid idea."

Ring.

"Hello?"

"Oh, hi! I...uh, this is Corey. Corey Kneedler."

There was great excitement in the tone of her response. We were both on cloud nine in that moment. It had been over 17 years since we'd last spoken.

But then something peculiar happened.

The more we talked, the less engaged I found myself in the conversation. We discussed everything under the sun, but we quickly realized that we had very little in common. Our political views were the opposite, views on abortion totally different, etc.

When I said goodbye to her, I was quite honestly a bit disappointed.

Was it because of my high expectations? This dream I'd been building in the back of my mind for so many years? Was the hype too much to live up to?

Devon and I never spoke on the phone again. In fact, after a brief conversation online shortly after that, we parted ways, and haven't spoken since.

To this day, I have absolutely no desire to speak with her, and I'm sure she feels the same about me. Last I heard, she was happily married and living the American dream. And that's great. But why don't I feel this void in my heart where she would fit perfectly into? Why isn't my world completely shattered, knowing that she and I didn't end up together?

For years I struggled with this. I wondered why something so fantastical could have happened (the email out of nowhere), only for it to end in disappointment. What was the purpose of it? What sort of hidden meaning could I find in all of it? Why did this happen to me?

But I guess what it boils down to is, that's life. Life isn't always about dreams fulfilled and fantasies realized. Not every fairy tale has a happy ending. And you know what? That's okay. If any lesson was to be learned here, it's that there isn't always a lesson to be learned.

Cherie

I love the taste of wine on your lips, but tonight the only thing I can taste is my own tears.

I can hear the cold rain coming down outside my window creating soft melodies, but all I can think of is the night we sang together in your car, discussing the differences between melody and harmony.

My pillow feels cold. My heart can't calm down and I can't sleep.

I'd rather hear the sound of your voice, feel the warmth of your body against mine, and touch your soft skin.

I'm a million miles away but I swear when I close my eyes I can still see you here, still smell your perfume, still hear you whispering "I love you."

Fate can be a cruel thing, and I often find myself wondering why I'm lying here alone.

What keeps me going on nights like this is memory, remembering what you taste like, remembering those beautiful eyes gazing into mine, the way your messy hair tickles my cheeks when we kiss, that sound you make when I hold you tight, the way that red lingerie looks on your incredible figure, the way you sass me when you're buzzed,

The way you love me.

Damn, I miss you.

It's only been 24 hours but it feels like an eternity.

It's not always easy, and sometimes the ocean between us feels so vast, but some nights I feel closer to you than I ever have.

Waiting is one of life's cruelest endeavors, but

I'd wait an eternity more if it meant spending one lifetime with you, my love.

As the hours pass and life brings rain, sun and snow, I'll be looking forward to watching every season change with you while we share those red wine kisses together.

Until then I'll keep loving you with all my heart, missing you like crazy and giving all of me to you.

It's cold outside but my heart is forever warm because of you.

Nights like these only make me long for you more passionately, feel you more intensely and love you more deeply.

I'll see you soon, valentine.

"This is what I hope for: a hallway filled with open doors, comfort from this silent war, a world where beating hearts hurt no more." — The Ghosts

Youthful Requiem

These lipstick stains still burn like fire, reminders of forbidden desire.

Never thought these chains could ever be broken.

All it took was one word of betrayal to be spoken.

Your lips always had a funny taste to them.

Now I know what it tastes like; now I know the bitter flavor of sin.

Now I'm sitting in a room full of strangers, wallflowers and head bangers wondering why I'm here.

Oh that's right, I'm trying to conquer my fear of shedding more tears.

You were the one who finally wrecked me, left me to drown in love's savage seas.

What's a man left to do when the writing on the wall spells out nothing but doom and gloom?

I hate you more than you could ever know.

You were the one seed I wish I'd never sewn.

But I can't stop thinking about you. Here I go again, picturing you in that sexy shade of blue.

What's wrong with me? I know better, but my body craves just another taste. What I wouldn't give right now for you to make my heart race.

My flesh is weak, and it weakens more with every pleasure that I seek.

For you I'll admit defeat, but only because my heart still needs to eat.

You tasted better than any dessert I've ever tried. You were worth every prayer, every wild party, every mistake, and every lie.

There's a whole buffet out there from which I could choose, but you're the only morsel I want to chew.

I feel like a wild animal trapped in a cage, ready to escape this zoo.

I wish I could say that we're through.

And I hate to say this..

But I don't think anyone could ever replace you.

"There is no refuge from memory and remorse in this world. The spirits of our foolish deeds haunt us, with or without repentance."
-Gilbert Parker

The Mother's Day Blunder

When I was in fourth grade my teacher announced that we'd be writing poems about our mothers for Mother's Day. Somehow I missed the part where she explained that the best poems would be selected to read on the local radio station. No big deal, right? Except in my world, Murphy's Law plays a pretty major role.

Not knowing what implications my poem may have, and assuming that no one else would read it but the teacher, I wrote the sappiest poem imaginable, describing how my mother "comforts me when I am sick," and "works so hard to put food on the table for us." She did all of those things of course, as any mother should do I suppose, but I hammered it up pretty good just to impress my teacher and hopefully score an easy A+. When I had finished my "masterpiece," I handed it in and didn't think about it again. That Friday our teacher announced to the class that the winner of the poem contest for our class had been chosen. "Wait, what? What contest?" I thought to myself.

Then she called out my name in front of the entire class. "Congratulations, Corey! You get to read your poem on the radio!"

"I...what???"

The class started clapping, and my face turned beet red.

"This uh, doesn't mean that anyone has read the poem, does it?" I thought.

Well it was too late. In a few days my poem was going to be heard by everyone in Coffeyville, in all its sappy glory. This can't be happening to me, surely I'm stuck in a horrible dream. Why me, God? Why??

That Saturday my mom took me to the local radio station, where I nervously clenched in my hands the poem I'd written. This was it. My life was all over. I'd never get a girlfriend again. My friends were going to nickname me "Sappy."

As I stepped into the recording booth goosebumps formed all over my arms, sweat poured from my forehead and I took a big gulp.

"Ok Corey, go ahead and read your poem," the DJ told me.

So I started reading it.

"My mom is the best mom because she comforts me when I am sick..."

"Oh wait, hang on a minute Corey. We uh.. messed up. Can you try it again?" the DJ abruptly told me.

So I started reading it again. This time I finished it, and miraculously didn't flub any words up.

The day was over and the deed had been done. I was ready to get the heck out of there and go home and bury my face in a pillow for the rest of the day.

As I stated before, Murphy's Law comes into play pretty often for me. And this time it got me pretty good.

The next day the poems were read on the radio, and of course my entire family was excited about it, telling me how proud they were of my "amazing accomplishment." My parents and grandparents recorded the reading of the poem on cassette tape, forever cementing this horrible memory in my mind.

Several kids from other grades read their poems, and everything was going perfectly, until it came to my poem.

What was heard was first the poem that I read, followed by the DJ saying, "And that was Corey Kneedler from four...." and suddenly the DJ was interrupted by my voice in the background, repeating "My mom is the best mom because she comforts me," "My mom is the best mom because she comforts me," "My mom is the best mom because she comforts me," in a loop, over and over again.

"Uh... yeah... that was...uh.....Corey...Kneedler..." the DJ said in a confused tone, while clearly frantically trying to figure out what the problem was.

And then it repeated again. About seven times; while the DJ nervously tried to figure out what was going on. After a loud "thump," it finally stopped, presumably thanks to the DJ's fist pounding onto the recording deck in frustration.

And the best part? It was all gloriously captured on cassette.

The whole thing couldn't have been more embarrassing.

How could I possibly go back to school on Monday? How could I bear to face my peers after such a horrific incident? What would they say? What kind of awful nicknames would they throw at me? "Comfort boy?", "Mommy's little baby?" "The Looper?"

The next Monday, I was a nervous wreck as I hobbled into Garfield Elementary School. I remember looking around at all my fellow students, studying carefully their glances, wondering when the first missile of criticism would be fired at me.

I made it into my classroom, and sat down at my desk, expecting the worst.

This was it. Any moment now, the classroom would explode with laughter and my classmates would heap hot coals of intimidation upon me.

But you know what? That never happened. Because, as it turned out, fourth graders don't actually listen to the radio. At least not in 1994. There were better things to do, like watch Power Rangers, pull their sister's pig tails, torture ants with a magnifying glass or ride their bikes across town for hours without informing their parents about it, which, believe it or not, kids actually did back then.

So that was it. No one seemed to notice the radio flub. No one seemed to care. My life had been spared. I thanked Jesus about a hundred times that morning for sparing me the embarrassment of a lifetime.

As for the tape, well.. it still exists somewhere, a reminder of an infamous Mother's Day flub that caused a nine year old boy to nearly wet himself with worry on a hot day in May 1994.

Because this incident truly shook me to my very core, since that day I have sworn to never truly apply myself to anything I write, only writing things half-heartedly, in fear that if I truly use my brain to create something amazing, I will once again be forced to read it on the radio.

Ok, so I made that last part up. It is still a terrifying thought though.

"For years I ran from the darkness.
Then I turned around and faced it. Now
I am the darkness." – The Ghosts

Transmission

"One of the most tragic things I know about human nature is that all of us tend to put off living. We are all dreaming of some magical rose garden over the horizon instead of enjoying the roses that are blooming outside our windows today." - Dale Carnegie

If you're receiving this transmission, it means I'm probably long gone, lost in some distant galaxy. Don't be alarmed. It's been very peaceful out here. Even loneliness feels different compared to earth. There's so much room in the vastness of space, so many beautiful lights as far as the eyes can see.

No, I wasn't alone. Not at all. If you could see it with your own eyes, I mean..all those heavenly bodies out there, if you squint your eyes just right they look like angels.

Is this what heaven looks like? Because I can't imagine it being any more beautiful than this.

It's almost made me forget about our tragedy a month ago, when things went haywire. Briggs took his last breath about 22 hours ago. Hayden, bless her heart..she hung on as long as she could, but she knew it was time.

She asked me for a kiss, you know. "Since I'm not going to kiss my husband goodbye, I want to close my eyes and kiss you and pretend it's him, if that's ok?"

I'm no substitute for her husband, a gold medal swimmer, Navy Seal, awesome father of four. But for a dying woman's last wish I suppose it couldn't have hurt. No, especially since my time is limited here, too. As I transmit this message I'm guessing I've only got maybe an hour left at best. I guess I'm the lucky one here. I've got no one left on earth to say goodbye to. Don't suppose you have a whole lot left to worry about when your family's all gone. Makes it easier knowing that when I pass, I'll just be reunited with them again.

Man, just think. Whatever's ahead is supposed to be more glorious than this. Have you ever seen the Milky Way before? Well, I suppose in pictures you have. But if you could see it with your own two eyes out the window of a spacecraft...man,

that's a real sight to behold. All those swirling lights out here in the pitch black void, it's like time stands still when you're staring at it. Makes you feel small, but at the same time so significant. Here I am, the only breathing creature for probably thousands and thousands of miles, and out there.. well, who knows what's out there?

I'd like to think that someone, some being out there is in the same boat right now. And he or she is just as in awe of the universe as I am.

God, what a great life. What a legacy to leave behind. I'm thankful. I really am. It was worth it. All of it.

When you get this transmission, I hope it finds you well. I hope..you've found peace somehow.

Oh, but I suppose you won't, will you?

Because you blew it all up, didn't you?

You'd finally had enough of each other, so you pushed the button. You let your jealousy get the better of you. Let your greed take hold, and as you demanded more and more, the world gave you less and less back.

Brother against brother, country against its people. You fought one another, but it didn't do any good. You waged war over oil, but it didn't help anything. Countless gallons of Innocent blood was spilled - and for what?

I suppose it's always been that way, hasn't it?

We've always been so self-absorbed, we never took the time to really appreciate what we had.

Never truly loved our fellow brothers and sisters like we should have. We had it all but didn't realize it. Now it's all gone.

Reminds me of a poem I read when I was younger:

"The world has given us a new mission: to collide like nuclear fission.

We'll strike each other down in the streets while little children hide under their sheets.

It was we who caused this, and it's too late to reverse it.

This is the world we live in.

A world conquered by sin.

A world we no longer want to live in."

A world we no longer want to live in indeed.

Because it's gone. All of it.

And my time here is almost over.

If anyone is out there, if by some miracle someone hears this, promise me you won't make the same mistakes we did. Promise yourselves that you'll set aside your own pride, your greed, your jealousy, and open up your eyes to the world around you.

You never know how much time you have left. Make every moment count.

My work here is done. I've run the good race, I've reached the finish line, and although my heart is still filled with regrets, I know I at least tried.

This is Captain James Reynolds, signing off for the last time. Good luck out there, wherever you are.

Elevator

As the elevator ascends, so too does my passion for you, my love.

Floor by floor, my body craves you more and more.

Floor one and we've just begun.

It's 3 a.m. but there's still plenty of time for fun.

Floor two, just me and you. Lips meet, hearts collide.

By floor five the fiery passion is alive,

pulling you close to me and drinking from your lips.

Floor 8 and I can't hardly wait to take you into

the bedroom and pounce on top of you and open up your gate.

Floor ten, the love making begins. We couldn't wait.

I lost control of my senses right after floor eight.

Floor 11 and we are in heaven. I'm riding hard on top of you and I

could never stop as I rip off your shirt and your chest comes into view.

Floor 13 and you're my queen. Such a beautiful scene unfolding on

the elevator floor, and you and I want more, more, more.

Floor 15 and you don't want to put on your jeans.

The destination is coming but I can't stop exploding inside you.

Floor 17 and I'm still making you scream.

You drop the F bomb and call out my name,

our hearts connected and passion still aflame.

Floor 20 and we've managed to somehow stand up and

I'm looking at the beautiful, irresistible woman I'm front of me.

I don't want this elevator to stop. I don't want to get off.

I just want to be inside you and keep going all night until we pop.

Floor 21 and we've reached our destination.

The doors open and four pairs of eyes stare.

We don't even care.

We look at each other and grin.

And when we get to our room, we'll do it all over again.

Her

In sunlight's rays she sits gazing into long forgotten memories, lost in words of love's unending crusade.

How delicate her hand rests between my palm, how painless does my heart feel

Whenever she brings that calm.

I would never desire to feel another's touch, because she's the woman that I love so very much.

Love in the Age of COVID-19

We fell in love in an age of pandemic. We found each other in a world of fear and uncertainty.

How can we love if we can't touch? How can we share dreams when we can't share the same space? If we remove this barrier, will the risk be worth it? Will our love flourish, or will this virus thrive on our foolishness?

If only I could kiss your lips, if only I could hold you tightly in my arms, I'd take you to a world so far away from here-- far away from the censorship, the deaths, the sense of helplessness. We'd strip away these hideous masks and dance on the moon, fly through the rings of Saturn, bathe in stardust and catch a ride on a shooting star.

But here on Earth is where we remain.

Your eyes have never looked so beautiful. Your hair never looked such a gorgeous shade of black. Even when the shadows of death and panic loom over us, I see things in you I never noticed before. Even when the world crumbles around us, I'll remain your rock, as you are mine. Not even the seemingly endless blare of ambulance sirens can drown the drums of our beating hearts.

What if the whole world had to take a step back from one another? What if everyone had to take a good look at each other? Do you think they'd see what we see when we stare into each other's eyes? Do you think they too would feel a deeper love for one another?

We won't let this virus stop us. We won't let the threat of death destroy our love. We will not be erased from the pages of this story called "life."

This sickness may defy borders, but our love defies time. If taking a deep breath and filling my lungs with the air outside takes me, then with my final breath I'll whisper through the fibers of this thin veil how much I love you.

Where

I felt it again today, that indescribable feeling that only comes once in a blue moon.

Sometimes I wonder if that feeling is the tapping of our young fingers on our shoulders, reminding us to keep living.

Days come and go, the seasons change and the earth turns.

But neither the wind nor the rain can ever erase the memories we made together in the atmosphere.

Like permanent markers, they remain on the fabric of time itself, unfading testaments to a time when the world was splashed with brighter colors.

We never really go away, do we?

Our bodies grow, our brains expand with knowledge, leaving little room left for imagination, but our souls remain the same.

It's a shame we left our sense of wonder in those woods, scattered under fallen branches and dissolved in flowing creek waters.

Trading the green for gray, the soft earth for pavement, the sweet smell of honeysuckle for clouds of diesel, we buried those innocent dreams under the weight of our own worries and fears, wrapped in blankets of stress.

Somewhere back there, in some moment of time we're still there, soaking our hands in cold flowing waters, counting clovers, balancing on mossy logs and slaying dragons with sticks.

Can you hear our young voices calling out to us?

"Come play with us," they shout.

They wonder why we grew up and left them behind so many years ago.

"We've been waiting for you all this time. Come, there are still more adventures left for us to find!"

What are we waiting for?

Let's go back to the place where death couldn't find us, where the darkness of the world couldn't creep in, the sanctuary of dreams that we built with our imagination.

Our kingdom awaits.

It's not too late.

The angels can wait just a little longer.

"There aren't enough stars in the sky, not enough crashing waves to listen to, not enough letters to write, not enough shapes in the clouds to measure up to the heights your love brings me to." – The Ghosts

Snapshot

Another innocent night spent looking into the mirror. Short shorts, revealing peach tank top, freshly straightened hair, mascara, wide eyes, face brushed with concealer, cherry-red lipstick. Ready.

Phone held high, angle just right.

Snap.

Smile at the screen, satisfied with what you've taken. It only took 272 tries.

Photo-edit-crop-filter-save.

Satisfied? Of course.

The picture of perfection. A snapshot of pure American beauty.

Add story-select photo-posted.

Head hits the pillow, alarm set. Roll over, pull the covers tightly. Smile.

Next morning the likes will flood in. The comments will be filled with horny boys gushing over your sexy persona.

Young and beautiful. No tomorrow, only today. And today is all that matters.

Wake up.

Wheelchair, darkened room. Pungent odor. Screams heard down the hallway. Who are you? Where are you? Bony fingers brush through brittle hair, jaw drops. Index finger pressed against sunken cheeks, trace the wrinkles. Hand to chest, sagging breasts.

Shock.

The sound of machines whirring. Cold.

It's so cold in here.

Dusty picture frames propped up on shelves. Scattered memories from where? From when? With whom?

Wheel yourself over to the mirror.

Horror.

No comments. Zero likes. Only loneliness. Where did time go?

Where did you go?

Push the panic button. Push the panic button. Panic. Panic. Panic...

"She brought life into this world, but she could never for the life of her gain his respect." – The Ghosts

Pompeii

Beneath the waves the ghosts of the wreckage are crying.

Meanwhile on the shore the young folks are dying.

Under the water the bodies extend their arms toward the surface.

On the beach, blood pours from every orifice.

The ghosts have seen it all before, they've witnessed this macabre ceremony.

And now the young souls of the fallen are taking one last glimpse of their crumbling city.

Soon two generations will gather together under the moonlight.

Soon the demons all around them will be dancing with delight.

Canvas

If I could rip my heart right out of my chest and use it to paint a picture, what would that picture look like?

Would the canvas merely show smeared blood across a blanket of white nothingness, or would you see us holding each other on cold winter nights?

Would the scene be filled with crimson stains of regret, brokenness, betrayal, and fear? Or would you see two souls dancing on a blanket of snow?

"It took an entire lifetime to find you, but only a few moments to lose you." — The Ghosts

Beautiful Hell

What hurts the most is the way you went out. Not with a whimper, a clap of thunder, or even a shout.

The crunching of the glass, fragments scattered like shards of ice covering the grass. The puncturing of the brain, blood, and innards soaking on wet pavement in the evening rain.

A mangled mess of blood and bone, unrecognizable to anyone you'd ever known.

Why did you go in such a fashion?

Young and beautiful one moment, unrecognizable in just a fraction.

Why do we leave this world in such terrible ways? Why does God allow us to go out with such morbid displays?

All I can remember is the way you were when I saw you lying in a pool of blood on the car's floor.

That image will forever haunt me, a vision of you I never imagined I'd see lying there in front of me.

Can hope be found in pools of crimson blood? Can closure be attained with memories of broken glass and metal stuck in the mud?

I want nothing to do with memories such as these. I don't want to dwell on thoughts of the one I love lying in that cracked pavement hell.

I hope to see you one day in heaven complete once more, your beautiful body no longer broken and mangled on the floor.

I promise to do my best to live a life worthy of heaven so I can join you one day in your beautiful eternal rest.

Go

When will you realize that it's not the size of a diamond ring that could make you sing?

When will you see that it's what's inside of you that makes you shine?

Don't let the world tell you that you are anything less than amazing. Prove to them that you could be absolutely anything.

You're worth more than gold, a light shining in the darkness, even when you grow old.

I know he broke your heart, but now it's time for a brand new start.

No one is holding you back but you. Time to plant a new seed and watch your life bloom.

You may not see it yourself, but your beautiful soul shines through day by day. You've touched this world in your own special way.

Wake up from your slumber. Wake up and see a world filled with wonder.

Rise up, take what you deserve and leave the cares of yesterday in the dirt.

No one can define who you are but you. Stop letting the past mold you and start anew.

I know there's a brighter future waiting out there for you.

As surely as the waves crash on the shore day after day, as surely as the sun sets and the moon rises, you're going to find your way.

You may think I'm wrong, but this isn't just another sad love song.

You deserve all that this world has to offer, whether you feel it or not. Your mind may keep spinning but the beating of your heart won't stop.

A better life is waiting, you just have to take that first step. Is it going to be hard at first? You bet.

But you can do it, and it's going to be worth it. Wouldn't you rather be happy than to be stuck forever in this pit?

Take a chance and spread those wings. Let the rest of the world have those diamond rings.

You were meant for more, a higher calling. You'll stand tall while the rest of the world is falling.

It's in the cards, you've got the best hand. Life's a stage, so strike up your band. Rock their faces off, rock the whole land.

It's all waiting for you, if only you'll decide to take that first step and finally hit your stride.

Even if it's you against the world, that's completely fine. You'll show them all, it's just a matter of time.

Trust me and you'll see, once you finally realize that you are truly free.

"She has convinced herself that she loves him because she doesn't feel like she deserves any better." — The Ghosts

Going out with Grace

She always looked radiant when she smiled; the tone in her voice was always so sweet when she'd ask me to stay for a while.

Her name was Grace, and her name was befitting of such a special woman whose love and affection one could feel with each and every soft embrace.

She was the last of the pure hearts, a beautiful sonnet in four parts.

If such beauty existed elsewhere, I couldn't seem to find it here nor there, nor anywhere.

When she'd walk into a room, her stunning beauty was comparable to purple mountain's majesty.

This world was blessed to have her. If only we'd been given a little more time with her, at least a few more winters.

Now she's lying in a casket four feet off the floor, loved ones passing by as they mourn.

They tried as hard as they could to piece her broken visage back together, but the attempt was futile after they pulled her from inches of inclement icy weather.

She died as she lived, entering that white void, painting pictures with her blood onto nature's cold blank canvas.

When they found her car on the side of the road, only the tail lights were visible, not far from the tracks of the railroad.

The ice and snow had preserved her body well. Little did the forest life know that there was such beauty resting among them in that icy hell.

Underneath her fur-trimmed box-quilted coat, she was dressed in a plaid A-line skirt with a white button-down blouse, and in her pocket, a hand-written note.

The handwriting was mine. The message was an attempt to explain why I had left her to be with Coraline.

As I look down at her face and say my final goodbye, tears fill my eyes, knowing my heart has fallen from Grace.

It was me who caused this great tragedy, caught up in my own sinful lust and creating such calamity.

Now I'll never see Grace smile again, forever haunted by the day I decided to walk away from an angel and chase after the lustful allure of my own sin.

A Writer's Lament

Is it a story I see on the page in front of me, or a picture I've imagined from inked black letters on a white page?

How would I know if my mind wasn't right? How could I be certain that these words are not spoken from my own insanity?

If I could open the top of my skull and reach in with my fingers, what would I feel? If I squeezed my brain as hard as I could, would words of truth drip out onto the page, or mere splotches of a madman's scattered thoughts?

Perhaps there are two of me. Perhaps my muse controls me. Or do I control my muse? Who's to say?

When you choose to dance with your own mind, you never know what kind of music will play. Am I swaying to a symphony of sweet harmony or an aria of sorrow?

Back and forth these thoughts travel, sometimes dark, other times filled with light.

Balance.

The wise say keeping life in balance is the key to happiness.

Today my thoughts are filled with romance, of nostalgic happiness coated with sugar and buttercup petals. Tomorrow my mind will be full of dread, focused on the macabre darkness humans hide so deep beneath their sheets at night.

I must share all of it. My heart and mind are compelled to tell their stories, weaving the darkness and the light together like a beautiful tapestry that portrays human life not as it is perceived by others, but by its ugliness, painted with the colors of insecurity and fear, with familiar patterns of dark sins perfectly balancing out the blanket composed of light and solace.

What does any of it mean?

Don't ask my mind, for it can't comprehend. Don't listen for answers in my voice, for it cannot speak truth.

The revelations you seek will be found not from the ink of a pen or the lips of mortals. Rather, they will be discovered in the howling of the wind at night, through the sound of those ancient spirits whispering melodies of wisdom into your ears while you sleep. Hold still and listen to the sound of their voices - those who have passed before us are calling to you, warning you never to make the same mistakes they did so long ago.

If only we still had ears left to listen, voices left to impart truth, or eyes to see what's been right in front of us for so long.

It's not madness to observe, not insanity that compels us to share the failures of these ghosts of home. It is the love of the spirits that still burn eternally in this terrestrial atmosphere, calling out to us day by day, guiding us and showing us which steps to take.

Heed their calling. These ghosts of home are forever restless, waiting for ears that can still listen, eyes that choose to see, and lips that are willing to speak truth.

One day when I'm long gone from here, you'll find me conversing amongst the ghosts of home, where my thoughts will carry onward through the words taken from my once mortal hand.

When I'm gone, don't look for me in a cemetery, and don't look to the clouds or in old photographs.

Read the words I've written, and you'll find me there. You'll find my truth.

"Sometimes you don't need to be healed to move forward. Sometimes the healing comes from moving forward." – The Ghosts

Down

I'm sorry my brain isn't working today.

I've been struggling to think since the blue skies faded to gray.

Life was once a piece of cake, my feet planted firmly on the ground whenever it would shake.

Now I'm not sure how much more devastation I can take.

It's 3 a.m. and I'm having trouble sleeping again.

I can't help but wonder if things would be different if I'd opened up the locked box I've kept my heart in.

Memories fade as I get faded, rationality choked out with every joint smoked.

Can hope be found in putrid clouds? Does truth hide behind our decaying burial shrouds?

I'm sick inside, God help me to fight. I can no longer think on my own, can no longer decide.

I hope I can figure it out before it's too late.

I want to love, but the biggest part of me is still filled with hate.

What a terrible fate.

Moonshot

The world sees a man lying in a bed, hooked up to machines that make him breathe.

The world sees an empty shell of a human being drooling onto his pillow.

But when I look at the man lying down with his eyes glazed over, I see you, dad.

I know you're still there. I know you're still you.

Somewhere behind that expressionless gaze you're thinking, "it sure is good to see you again, son."

I swear sometimes I can hear you whispering to me how proud of me you are between the gasps of breath you take.

You're in there somewhere. I can feel you when I grab your hand. You never really went away, did you?

What's it like in there? Does it feel like being trapped in a box? Like a genie trapped in a lamp for a thousand years, hoping one day to be released again?

Is it comfortable where you are?

I hope so, dad.

I hope you're not suffering. I hope you still feel the warmth of my love passing though you when I kneel down beside you and pray for you. I hope the words I speak to you somehow find their way to wherever you are, and they bring you some kind of joy.

I've tried for years to figure out why this happened to you. Why life could be so cruel, why a loving God would allow this.

But I finally realized I could spend the rest of my life being angry about it, or I could choose to be at peace, knowing you're still here.

Sure, you may not be able to throw the baseball to me in the backyard any more. You can't read bedtime stories to me or assure me everything is going to be ok when it's storming outside, can't take me to Tasty Freeze to get me an ice cream before supper without telling Mom, can't carry me in your arms through the flooded creek behind our old house.

But somewhere, you're still reminiscing about the good old days, still thinking about those sun-kissed baseball summers we shared, still laughing about the pranks we used to pull on grandpa together, and still smiling the way you used to when mom would give you a big warm hug after you'd get home from work.

I know someday you'll wake up again, dad. Whether in this life or the next.

Either way, I'll be waiting for you on the other side with open arms. Neither time nor distance nor silence can keep us apart, dad.

Forget what the world sees. Forget what science and the medical field sees.

I see my dad lying right there. My role model. My hero.

I still have my old baseball glove we used to play catch with. It's sitting on my fireplace mantle as it has for many years now, with the Ken Griffey, Jr. autographed baseball sitting in it.

One of these days dad, we're gonna take that down from the shelf and play some catch.

And when we do, we'll catch up on old times together.

You think they play baseball in heaven, dad?

I think so.

Someday you and I are gonna make the World Series look like a tee ball tournament.

I'll wait up for you. I promise.

"When you see the moon, does it glow brightly for you too? When you think of me, does my radiant love come into view?" — The Ghosts

Spider

The spider clings to the floor motionless as if it's terrified to move.

"I see you over there, buddy."

Bathroom floor, 3:25 a.m.

John has been lying there since 8:29 p.m. after a sudden spell of dizziness before collapsing to the floor.

John can't move. He feels paralyzed from the waist down. The 85-year-old man lives alone in a tiny apartment on the 14th floor.

"Just you and me, pal. Looks like neither of us is getting out of this one easily."

The spider remains static, seemingly staring with respectful fear at the giant lying two feet away.

"Looks like this is it for me, my friend. This is how it ends, lying on the floor with a little spider as my final companion."

The spider listens to John pour his heart out as he recalls memories from the days of his youth, reminiscing about falling in love with his wife, the day his children were born, the day his mother passed away, and the worst day of his life - when his beloved wife took her last breath.

"You know, one of my biggest fears was to die alone. Thank God I've got you here to watch me go. For what it's worth, I'm thankful for you my friend."

John's lifeless body was found 27 days later, rotting on the bathroom floor. A spider web had been formed around his face.

The spider had laid eggs inside his left eye socket. Her babies were crawling all over him when he was found.

The spider and her family had found a new home inside John. She was thankful he stuck around a while.

Time

Foreword

If we can't learn lessons from our past, then what meaning can we give to our future? What hope can we truly have if we continue down life's path without taking time to reflect on what has shaped us into the men and women we've become?

Life passes by so quickly. Don't forget to take the time to look back. Sometimes the answers to the questions you seek are in the fabric of times gone by. Focus, and you'll see a clear picture unfold before your very eyes.

I wrote this way back in 2008. It was one of the first stories I ever wrote. Of all the things I've written, this is one of the most important to me, and I find myself coming back to it time after time to remind myself of what life really means and why it's still worth living.

The story

September 9. Late Afternoon. I step outside and a gentle breeze blows across my face. I close my eyes, and suddenly the past merges with the present.

I'm three years old. I'm in my backyard playing with my friend Devon. My dad has just raked up some leaves and we're going to jump into them. The gentle wind brings a perfectly mild temperature to our surroundings. She smiles at me. I smile back. We hold hands, close our eyes and jump in. Nothing else matters to us right now - we're living in this fun moment.

I'm four years old. My mom has taken me to my friend Jeffery's house. We're standing outside. The wind carries leaves across our feet. He shows me his new action figure. "Wow, this is so cool!" I say to him. He looks at me and smiles. "You can have it if you want it," he says. I'm shocked. I've wanted this action figure for a long time. Is this what it means to be a friend?

I'm five years old. I'm sitting down on Devon's doorstep crying. She and her family have just moved away. I feel all alone. I can hear my mom's voice in the distance calling me home. I don't feel like going back home. I just want to sit here and cry.

I'm seven years old. My friend John and I are putting the finishing touches on our Ghostbusters gear. We're going to capture some ghosts. On the nearby stereo a cassette tape plays "On Our Own" by Bobby

Brown. This is our time. We're on top of the world. Nothing can stop us. Nothing.

I'm eight years old. I'm on the phone with John and my eyes are full of tears. He's moving to Texas. It's hard to talk to him. For the first time since I've known him it's hard to find words to say.

I'm nine years old. My friends Eric and Brad want to go bike riding. I don't really like hanging out with these guys. Yesterday we rode into my neighbor's yard and he yelled at us. It was their idea, not mine. I don't trust them. I'm not a trouble maker like they are.

I'm ten years old. I'm at church with my friends Caitlin, Landon and Dalton. We're watching a 1984 Super Bowl halftime show on video, laughing hysterically. Surely good times like this will never end.

I'm 12 years old. I'm sitting in my sixth grade classroom. The teacher opens up the window and a nice, cool breeze blows in. I'm sitting two desks away from Sara, the girl I have a crush on. I'm too shy to tell her that I like her though. She keeps looking over at me. Does she like me? No. Surely not. But what if she does? Then what do I do? I feel an anxious feeling of happiness welling up inside of me.

I'm 13 years old. I'm sitting in front of a campfire holding my girlfriend's hand. I look over at my friend and he doesn't look very happy. For a moment I feel bad for ditching him, but then I look into her eyes and that feeling disappears instantly.

I'm 16. I've ditched my friends tonight to hang out with my girlfriend. My friends hate her. Who cares? I don't need them anyway. She and I are sitting on her bed listening to music. She puts on some vanilla sugar-flavored lip gloss. I know where this is going. I'm nervous, but anxious. This is our first kiss together.

I'm 17 years old. She wants more from me now. We've been going in the wrong direction for months now. I'm not giving her what she wants. I can hear her crying as I'm walking out the door. As I open the door to my car I can hear her begging me to come back. I start the car. I'm driving away and not looking back.

I'm 19 years old. I'm talking to my new girlfriend Joana on the phone. We're making plans to see each other. Just a few more months, and we'll be together forever. I can't wait. Life is so exciting right now. I've finally found the right one.

I'm 20 years old. I have just ended the worst relationship in my life. I haven't slept for two days. My body feels weak, my stomach in a knot. I'm looking out my apartment window. She's finally leaving. This nightmare is finally over. My hands are shaking. I never want to see her again. I fall to the floor, hands to my face. God, is it really over?

I'm 20 years old. I'm standing next to the river. In my right hand I'm holding a ring. My heart is burning with anger. In my anger I throw the ring into the river with all my might. The ring sinks to the bottom of the river, and with it, my memories of her. From this moment I can finally move on.

I'm 21. I'm sitting in my apartment writing a story for a magazine. I'm trying to convey through words what I've learned over the years, if anything at all. Words fail me. I keep asking God for wisdom but nothing's coming to me. God, how much time have I wasted? Isn't there more to life than this?

I'm 22. I'm lying outside on a concrete bench looking up at the stars. It's a clear night. The breeze feels so good as it blows through my hair and my face. I'm pondering life, my existence, my purpose, what God's will is. I know He's there. I can feel Him all around me. Where are you, God? Show yourself to me.

I'm 23. Optimism fills my spirit as I take a deep breath outside tonight. It's getting colder day by day. Winter will be here soon, and my time of reflection will soon end. There's more to come on the horizon. For the first time I hear God speak to me.

"Haven't I taken care of you?" He says to me.

That's all I need to hear.

It's a beautiful evening.

It's going to be a beautiful life, too.

"Our bodies connect but our hearts flounder inside our chests. This cycle must be broken before it rips us to shreds." — The Ghosts

Frames

These old photographs are tearing down the walls inside of me.

Memories of the way life used to be.

Look how happy we looked in Kodachrome.

Sharing happiness together in the place we once called home.

This old photo album is like a tapestry of beautiful memories.

Those were the days. No guilt, no shame, no worries.

Where did it all go?

Was it buried beneath the years of snow?

Did the rain wash it all away, never to return another day?

Did we hide these memories away deep inside our minds to preserve them as this old world slowly unwinds?

Like a picture frame our memories hang, empty without relief, only pain.

There

Sometimes I can feel you blowing through my hair, that cool breeze tickling my ears, reminding me to breathe again.

The tapping in the hallway that awakes me in the middle of the night, reminding me that you're still there.

And in the morning when I pour a cup of coffee, the birds sing their beautiful songs outside the window, like a symphony you've composed just for me.

When the radio plays our song, I know it's no coincidence. When the neighborhood children's laughter echoes off the walls, I can hear you, like you'd just told one of your corny jokes.

Sure, the days get lonely sometimes. Sometimes I'll stare at your old La-Z-Boy and see you still sitting there, reading the evening newspaper.

I suppose I should be sad, but honestly there's no time for that any more. The kids call twice a week, the cats never stop eating, Mrs. Heady comes over fairly frequently to bring me some muffins or a casserole she's experimented with. No, I really don't have much to complain about, all things considered.

You and I, well…we've had our good years together. 62 whole years of wedded bliss. Well, mostly bliss. God knows neither of us were perfect, but we always made it somehow.

I suppose if that's what they call living, then it wasn't so bad. These golden years are only the end of a journey. And what does one do at the end of a long journey? Well, they rest.

Even God Himself rested on the seventh day of creation. I figure I've earned a few days of rest after living for 84 years, raising two kids, working several jobs, keeping up with you and your crazy endeavors, and burning a lot of holiday dinners along the way.

I know you're still here to remind me that life is still worth living, no matter how bored I may get, no matter how frustrated I get with these tired old eyes trying to make out the letters on Wheel of Fortune. Even when these bony hands can't crochet any more, even when I've read my last book, I'll rest easy knowing that you're just waiting for me.

What more could I ask for? I met the love of my life, I spent the majority of my years with you, and even though you're gone now, I know it's only a matter of time before we pick up right where we left off.

And I know these subtle reminders I see and feel every day will carry me through any thoughts of loneliness that may try to creep into my mind.

So when the rain pours down and I can hear you opening the front door, when the thunder roars and I can hear you snoring, when the wind howls through the screen door and I can feel your gentle touch, it will make these passing hours a little more pleasant - until I see you face to face, and you hold me tightly in your arms again.

Youth of the Nation

We are still the Youth of the Nation.

We're still scared, clueless and unsure of the future. We are the bullied. We are the bullies. The future rulers of this world, the perfect mothers and fathers that our parents never could be.

We were supposed to have it all together by now.

But in so many ways, so little has changed.

A new element of fear was introduced to us in 1999, and it brought a difference to everything. Today, that element is a part of everyday life not just for us, but for all walks of life.

And we are still trying to figure out how to deal with that.

Were we the first generation charged with the responsibility of keeping these tragedies from happening? But what could we have done? We were scared, confused, and angry. It wasn't us. We didn't create this, did we? Surely our moms and dads taught us better. Surely we had more sense than that. We knew right from wrong. We were just awkward teenagers trying to find ourselves, trying to find our place in this world.

And yet it happened.

And it happened again.

And again.

And again.

And we screamed. We cried. We tried fighting it through poems, movies, songs, and memorial services.

And still, it continued.

We've shouted into the faces of politicians, held protests, waged wars of peace, taken guns away, preached the gospel to the lost.

And still, it continues.

What have we done wrong? What more can we do? Are we not angry enough? Have we not cried hard enough? Do we not love deeply enough?

We still haven't figured it out.

And I wonder, will we ever?

Was it we who started this? Was it our generation that caused the cracks in society, this unstoppable decay of morality?

Or was it our parents? Or their parents before them?

Maybe we will never really know. Maybe we won't ever figure it out. Maybe we are still exactly who we were 20 years ago. The scared, the confused, the angry Youth of the Nation.

"Knowledge is knowing that the tomato is a fruit, wisdom is knowing not to put tomato in a fruit salad" -The Ghosts

Futile

What did it feel like, Dr. Cranor, when your body was on its way flying down to the cold pavement below?

Did time stop just for a moment, allowing you to reflect on your life's mistakes? Did you think about your hopes and dreams? If you could rewind time, would you do it? Was it worth the energy it took to climb to the top?

A cat wanders the streets, crying out for attention among the passerby, none of which seems to take notice of the blood stains on its paws.

Was life better before, Dr. Cranor? Before all the stress, the physical pain, and the boring day-to-day routine? Was it only bad because you made it that way?

The owner of Doug's Bakery hears the cat's meows and looks down at it.

"What do you want, pal? Are you hungry?"

He throws a piece of a freshly baked roll down on the ground, but the cat pays no attention to it.

"Not good enough for you, eh? Fine, get out of here, you filthy twat!"

As you stood there, Dr. Cranor, looking down at the city streets below, I wondered what was going through your mind. Did you shed a tear? Was there a smile on your face?

A little girl is walking with her mother down the sidewalk, when she notices

the cat.

"Mommy, look at the kitty! Aww, he's so cute!"

As she reaches down to pet the cat, her mother interrupts her. "We need to keep moving, Cindy or we'll be late! Come on!"

The cat's eyes fill with despair as it stops and stares at the girl while her mother drags her away.

Does it really matter in the end, Dr. Cranor? Did they listen to your message? Does anyone really care what you've done? Is it worth it to just become another small blurb in the newspaper that will be forgotten by tomorrow? A life of prestige, only to end as a statistic?

The cat's meows seem to fall on deaf ears, as pedestrians pass it by one by one.

Was it your hope that they would feel sorry for you, Dr. Cranor? Or were you just giving up?

It's seven o'clock in the morning, and the birds are singing their songs, echoing off the walls of the downtown storefronts. People pass by unaware of the tragedy that lies mere feet away from them.

So much for dying with dignity. I hope it was worth it to you, my friend. I hope you've found whatever peace you were looking for.

Dr. Cranor's body lies in a pool of blood in an alley behind Deb's Boutique.

The cat returns to the scene and lies down next to him.

It would be another 45 minutes before he is discovered.

Dr. Cranor's obituary runs in the paper the next day. Most don't even notice it. A small accompanying piece is found at the bottom of the obituary page, telling of the Doctor's suicide.

Was it worth it my friend? Did you leave your lasting mark? Did you show them once and for all? Did you break their hearts like yours was broken?

Futile.

All of it was futile.

Now that you know, what will you do?

Goodbye

The other day, I returned to my childhood home for the first time in more than twenty years. What I discovered is that even though the physical walls remain, the memories have long since moved on to another place and time. I stood quietly in the empty living room, recalling countless happy memories from a life that seemed so long ago, so distant. In my path to adulthood, so much has changed since the days when I'd look down at my tiny fingers and count to ten. Now I look down at my hands and count the wrinkles and scars I've acquired over the years. As I stood there in that empty old house, I swore that if I listened carefully enough, I could still hear the laughter of my brother and I echoing off the walls. I could see the old oak finished TV set sitting there, displaying the silly antics of Bugs Bunny on

Nickelodeon. I could hear my mom's voice calling out to us, "Supper is ready!"

I couldn't help but wonder, where does time go? What happened to all these memories, this life that I once knew so long ago? Do these memories fade away into oblivion, or do they go somewhere special, waiting for us to relive them one day after we pass away? I'd like to believe the latter.

As far as I'm concerned, heaven would be just that - reliving all those old happy memories again.

Childhood comes and goes in the blink of an eye. We take it for granted while we're young, and it's only when life slows down and you look back that you truly appreciate what you had. And by that time you realize that no matter how hard you try, no matter what you do, you can't ever go back.

Life is cruel in that way.

I walked into the garage, where I could see my dad lying on his back, changing the oil in his car. I looked down at the concrete floor and gazed upon the countless stains that still remained, wondering how many of them my dad had left over the years.

Finally I walked upstairs to my old bedroom. Countless memories flooded my mind; memories of friends coming over, playing with action figures on the floor, playing house with the neighborhood girls, listening to the rhythm of the raindrops hit the window sill outside at night. It's all gone now, locked away somewhere deep in my mind, behind closed doors that are getting harder and harder to open as the years pass by.

My return to the old house was bittersweet to say the least. When I walked back out of the house I turned around and whispered, "Goodbye."

I realized that not only was I saying goodbye to the house, but also to youth, to innocence, to family members who have passed away, and to the memories of a life so long ago, lost somewhere in the passages of time.

There comes a point in one's life when you realize that the only thing left to hang on to from your past is the memories. Even objects held over from days gone by have no meaning without memories attached to them.

And loved ones....they come into our lives and then pass on, often before we take the opportunity to tell them how much we love them. We can only hold on to the living for so long. After that, our memories of them are all we have left. And as I grow older and my mind deteriorates, those memories begin to fade. Countless people over the centuries have tried so desperately to hang on to loved ones through many different methods. All have tried, and failed. The saddest part of losing loved ones is

I put this video together because one day this may be all I have left to remember those happy times. Consider this a portrait of my life, a brief moment in time, before life became complicated, before responsibility, before the worries of the world weighed down on us, before the sting of depression stung our hearts, before death's cold hands wrap around our necks.

I will watch this video, at various times in my life, to remind myself of the good times. To remind myself that, as a father now, while memories of my childhood begin to fade, I now have the opportunity to make new memories with my son, who will one day also look back and wonder where time went, where his childhood ran off to.

So I say goodbye to a life so long ago, to those I've loved so dearly along the way, and finally, to the memories that will one day fade from my mind.

Anatomy

What good is a beating heart if it's empty inside? What use is it, having eyes without opening them?

What good is a nose if you don't take time to smell the roses?

Why have ears if you refuse to listen?

Why touch someone if you don't feel anything?

Why hold your tongue when you can speak words as sweet as honey?

What use is a body without a soul?

What use is a brain without thoughts?

What will you do when each of these fades away?

What will you feel when there's nothing left to touch? Nothing left to see, hear or taste?

Empty

My heart lies six feet under. I've laid to rest what was left of the love that once burned so passionately inside me.

For so many years, I was the little boy standing on the street corner, holding his big beating heart out to those passing by.

"Excuse me, ma'am? Would you..."

But every time they'd walk away.

"Miss, I'd like to give this to you. I promise I.."

But every time I'd offer them my heart, I'd watch them walk right past me and fall into the arms of someone else.

There were times I wanted to pull it back, tuck it safely back inside my chest, close it off from the world. But I just couldn't. There was this burning desire inside me to love someone. Call it a flaw, call it a fool's pipe dream, but I was built for this. If only they'd give me a chance, I'd...

Well, I'd give them the world. I'd give them all of me and more than they could ever imagine. I'd hold them tightly in my arms every night and tell them how much I loved them. I'd pick them up when they fall, carry them through the fire, sacrifice all of me for them to feel loved and appreciated forever.

Every day I'd stand on that street corner, hoping and praying that someone would stop just long enough to notice me, maybe stand still long enough to hear the rhythm of my heart beating for them.

If only they'd listen, I'd shower them with my love, and maybe, just maybe…they'd shower me with their love as well.

But when the sun went down each evening, my heart was soaked not with the love of another, but with my own tears.

The storms came. The winds blew. The snow came. The bitter chill of winter saturated the land with ice. But still my heart kept beating.

Years passed, and I watched as friends, family and acquaintances found their angels, found true happiness and someone to share their hearts with.

But yet I remained, all alone.

On the same street corner I stood, the same little boy who never had a chance to grow up, never had a chance to feel loved or appreciated, holding my heart outward.

There were times I'd scream at the top of my lungs, "Someone please take this! Can't any of you hear me? Please!"

But no one seemed to hear my cries.

There were days I'd look down at it and think, "Maybe I'm just not good enough for anyone. Maybe I'm not worth it."

There were days I wanted to rip it apart and walk away. Sometimes I thought if I ended my own life they'd finally notice my lifeless corpse lying on the ground. Maybe then someone would see my heart lying on the sidewalk and finally pick it up.

But that was a foolish idea and I knew it.

One day I stood on the same street corner and gazed out into what once was a crowded city square, and realized something.

I was all alone.

The people had come and gone. They'd all found their special someone.

There was no one left.

I'd waited too long. Spent my whole life hoping and praying for something that I wasn't meant to have.

So I stepped down from the makeshift wooden podium I'd created, took one last look at my heart, and with tears streaming down my face, I decided to place it back into my chest.

I walked away feeling defeated, feeling worthless, feeling unwanted...

Unloved.

So I walked to the old cemetery where so many hearts had stopped beating so long ago.

I stood before an empty plot, taking a deep breath.

With my last ounce of strength I pulled my heart from my chest, and buried it.

I chiseled one final message for it into the tombstone.

"Here lies the biggest heart that ever beat, the greatest love that was never found," it read.

As time passed I learned to live without a heart. I grew up without caring, without longing, without hurting. I became a shell of a man, moving forward without ever having to hold my arms out for someone to love me ever again.

I became a spectator of the world around me.

I let life pass me by, and in time replaced the gap where my heart once resided with hatred. I lied, I cheated, I stole, and I hated. I hated with such intensity, broke as many hearts as I could, and never had remorse.

And yet, somewhere deep inside me, I was still the same little boy, holding his big beating heart for the world to see, hoping with all his might that one day someone might stop by and accept it, accept him for the scared, helpless but loving little boy he was.

Some people never grow up. Some are never given the chance.

Some hearts thrive by loving and feeling loved, some are protected and nurtured.

But some hearts die before their time.

It's too late for me, but perhaps it's not too late for you.

Is your heart still beating? Do you still desire to love? Don't make the same mistake that I made. Don't bury your heart, because you won't ever be able to get it back.

Hold on for another day if you can. That's when you'll find them. That's when they'll finally notice you and your hearts will connect like two lost souls finding one another at last.

It's not too late.

Love now, while your heart is still beating.

Soldier

May 1944:

Lord, forgive me, for I'll have to put my Christianity on hold for the remainder of this war. I ask for your divine grace for the things I will say, the actions I will take part in, the horrors these eyes will see;

The lives I will take.

In order to win this war, I'll need to become someone I've never been before. I'll have to become the one thing I've been terrified of becoming my whole life:

I'll have to become a man.

I pray you'll forgive me when mothers fall to their knees when they find out their sons have paid the ultimate price, when fathers don't come home to their little girls lying in bed at night waiting for them, when the chance for boys to become men is severed far too early because of my actions.

Forgive me when I try to turn off my heart as bloodshed spews all around me, when explosions rock the earth beneath me, when I hear the screams of my brothers lying in agony, knowing they can't be saved, that there is no hope left for them.

I may use profanity in the foxholes, I might curse your name as bullets pierce my flesh, I may question my own sanity when wiping the blood of my comrades off my face. But I won't give in to the darkness.

They can take my body, but my soul belongs to you.

How many families must be ripped apart before you're satisfied? How many rivers of blood do we have to wade through before the sacrifice is enough?

How many brilliant minds are being blown out on smoky battlefields? How many future doctors, scientists, preachers, and teachers are taking bullets to save our freedom?

Sometimes amidst all this chaos, I wonder if it's worth it.

Can you see it? Can you hear their cries for help? Can you feel the pain of thousands of human beings being simultaneously ripped apart at any given moment? Can you taste their tears as they watch helplessly as their closest friends get mowed down into piles of bloody meat?

My God, what's it all for? What's any of this for?

Lord, if all this death and destruction is truly your will, then let thy will be done.

But I don't agree with it.

How could I? How could any of us?

If I make it to the other side alive, I promise I'll try to make as much sense of it as I can.

But if I make it to the other side beyond flesh and blood, I hope you'll find a place for me up there, even after all the horrors I'm about to take part in.

I promise I'll do my best not to lose my head, lose my sanity, or lose my soul.

I ask for mercy for all of us, if you have any left to spare.

And when this is all over and we are all in pieces, I pray that somehow you'll put us all back together again.

You're History

Sometimes I can feel you out there, old friend. In the vapors of my mind I can see you standing there next to me with those goofy sideburns and that awkward, lanky figure. I can see you in your room, toiling away at an old video game, lying in bed dreaming about your latest crush, waking up in the middle of the night to take a swig of chocolate milk.

I can hear your laughter echoing off your bedroom walls as you and your friends share a really cheesy inside joke together.

I can hear the sound of Dad's voice shouting, "Ok boys, time to wrap it up. It's time for bed!"

I can hear the pecking of keyboard keys as you take part in naive discussions with someone on MSN Messenger in the wee hours of the morning.

I can feel the cool autumn breeze blowing through your bedroom window as the leaves rustle gently outside, slowly putting you into the deepest, most comforting sleep.

But most importantly I can feel your innocence. I can feel your young heart beating so strongly. The way it did before it acquired all these scars. Before that innocence was ripped away and you felt the cold sting of the world. Before all the tear-soaked pillows and frustrated punches into concrete walls. Before your heart was broken into a thousand pieces and then glued back together so many times.

Before the world fucked you over and left you on your own. Before loved ones betrayed you, killed themselves or lied to you.

Before laughter became as scarce as the rarest of metals, before religion stopped making sense, before churches quit preaching the truth. Before the world started fighting over senseless things, before the stars of our childhood movies started dropping dead one by one.

God, how I wish I could be there again sometimes, in my bedroom dreaming of days to come, chasing after that blonde-haired crush I had, listening to Eiffel 65 on a Sunday afternoon, sipping on some Mountain Dew without a care in the world.

I didn't know what I had back then. Didn't know how wonderful it was to be bored out of my mind with nothing to do. Took for granted the peace that surrounded me, the simplicity of everyday life, the lack of bills to pay, the security of knowing day to day that things were going to make sense when I woke up in the morning.

I know you're still out there somewhere, my old friend. I miss you. God knows I do. And one day we will be reunited again. I don't know how and I don't know when, but I look forward to that day. And when we are, we'll sip on some Mountain Dew again, maybe share a smile or two.

"Sad and lonely as I may be, I don't need your sympathy. I just need you to find me." – The Ghosts

Restless

Moonlight shines through the bedroom blinds as you wake from a restless dream.

Hands to face, wipe the nervous sweat from your forehead.

The distant sound of a train whistle carried by howling winds echoes through your ears.

Your mind is chasing memories of her again, at such a swift pace your tired mind almost feels like losing consciousness.

Get out of bed slowly with a tired groan, flip on the lamp on the bedside table.

"One last look," you tell yourself as you open the drawer filled with paper memories that grip so tightly to your heart but no longer hold any meaning to her.

Pick up that photograph of you two on the Ferris wheel.

As you hold it in your hand, you feel your heart sink deep into your chest.

Take a deep breath and a hard swallow, and rummage through numerous letters filled with hearts and empty promises written in cursive.

They're only pieces of paper now, stained with ink from years past - meaningless characters scribbled onto worn out wide-ruled parchment.

The thought of her lying in bed tonight in someone else's arms ignites an inferno of anger inside your rapidly beating heart.

Slam your fist onto the night stand, knocking over the lamp onto the floor.

It doesn't make you feel any better.

You swear you could slam your fist into a thousand walls, but it wouldn't mend the brokenness inside your heart.

Stand up slowly, unclench your right fist and stumble into the hallway; maybe a drink would do you some good.

Flip on the kitchen light.

Run your fingers through your unkempt hair, take a deep breath and reach for the bottle sitting on the counter.

Your arm doesn't quite make it to the bottle, as you suddenly collapse to the floor, knocking your head on the cabinet door on the way down. Black out.

Now dream of better days, dream of regrets, dream of hopelessness and dream of happiness.

Drown in your sorrows as they take you away to the darkest recesses of your mind.

And when you wake, the process will repeat, just as it always has.

Feelings as old as time itself.

As the clock ticks away, all through the world broken hearts wake to the same dissonant rhythm night after night. Lost dreamers hope for a better tomorrow, but it never meets them in the morning.

What is the meaning of all this suffering?

I don't know, but I promise we're going to figure it out one day.

Some day it'll all make sense.

Change

I've always been partial to change, always excited for a chance to rearrange.

I've always felt nostalgic for the tragic, weaving in and out of the bright lights of traffic, trying to keep my soul from going static.

Is there anything quite as beautiful as the ocean waves? In and out, they drizzle the beach with their aquatic gaze, shaping the sand and forcing it to change.

As far as I can see, there's nothing quite worse than age-old monotony. When everything stays the same, we start to forget where we are going or why we came.

I don't want to live my life in a way that's stagnant. Shooting for the stars, getting lost in my beautiful dreams is what I want.

Some say change is scary, whether it's starting a new job, moving to a new location or getting married.

I say change is a necessity, a thing we try to avoid with all our might, but it always finds a way to us eventually, even when it's not pretty.

Isn't there a good reason for the changing of seasons? Is not beauty found in every bird's musical sound, with every leaf or snowflake that hits the ground?

If you're looking for me, I'll be moving forward, hitting every high note and striking every chord. I assure you that where I'm going I will never get bored, so don't try to look for me while my heart and soul wander the woods and explore.

Change is on the horizon. Can you feel it coming?

If you listen carefully, you can hear the angels humming.

Backyard fantasy

When dad goes away, it's time for us to play.

It's safe now that he's gone. Time's a' wastin', and we've been up since dawn.

The afternoon sun is starting to peek through. The clouds are going away, and the sky is turning blue.

Come on sis, let's go outside and create our own world full of bliss.

Mom is still asleep, so it'll be a while before we can eat.

In the meantime, let's build ourselves a purple palace, go on an adventurous quest to find the holy chalice.

In our schooner let's sail the seven seas, floating endlessly with the sails blowing in the warm breeze.

We'll leave all our cares and worries behind. We don't need anyone or anything, just the imagination inside our minds.

In the world we create, there will be no more hate, no more fighting, no more screaming and no more biting.

In our world there won't be any alcohol – no, not a drop at all. There won't be any little white pills, just big, green beautiful hills.

The universe is our playground. Come on sis, it's time to go. Let's go adventure bound!

You'll wear a tiara and I'll wear a crown. We'll be the beloved rulers of our very own town.

Mr. Bear will be the sheriff, Miss Cupcake the mayor. And when trouble comes her way, we'll be the ones to save her.

We'll feast on cookies and pizza every day, and give toasts with glasses full of pink lemonade. We won't ever get too hot, because there will always be plenty of shade.

Mom and dad will never know, because we'll have our own secret world in which to grow.

A place where dad can no longer hurt us. Where we'll never again hear him cuss, never feel the sting of his belt, no more waking up with another new welt.

And when mom finally wakes, we'll be gone and it'll be too late.

We'll find our happiness elsewhere in a world that we create, a world that we'll both share, a world without any hate.

We'll find that world together, sis. You just wait and see. Whatever's ahead will be much brighter, even if it's just you and me.

Thoughts

Oftentimes I get lost in my thoughts, gazing up at the stars and connecting the dots.

Are these patterns forming a future that matters?

Will I be able to make sense of the astral tapestry that's been laid out in front of me?

Echoes of another time, from another place penetrate my thoughts and form ethereal rhymes.

Are these thoughts my own, or are they frequencies that were sent out eons ago from some place unknown?

Something is happening, the fabric of time is rearranging into dreams I keep imagining.

Is the creator's voice no longer silent? Has the chaos we've created awakened the sleeping giant?

Or has he always been there, silently gazing into this snow globe filled with toxic air that our lungs all share?

I'm only a man.

I have no strength to offer.

Why would He come running back to me after all those times I ran?

Like an orange, the world's layers are being peeled away, revealing our shameful display.

How rotten must our hearts become before we succumb to the beating of our own wicked drums?

What if we can't figure out how to become one before we are vaporized by the coming of the sun?

Sometimes I wonder.

Will we ever listen to the sound of the clapping thunder? Will we ever try to make sense of our own foolish blunders?

I can't say.

Either tomorrow will come or it won't. Who are we to ask for another day? Who are we to think things will always go our way?

I'd rather live as a human in need of a savior than ascend to such heights that I can't save myself from the consequences of my own misbehavior.

Time still passes. Some days like a speeding bullet, other days like molasses.

And here we are, still living, still breathing. Still time left for teaching.

Still time left for learning.

But most importantly, there's still time left for loving.

Is there anything greater than such a commandment?

I can think of nothing.

A Christmas Walk

It's a cold night. He can see his breath. The bitter chill of the wind makes his eyes water. His hands are tucked tightly in the pockets of his old ragged coat. He's walking down the sidewalk, passing the myriad of stores downtown. All the windows are illuminated with Christmas lights. Cars drive by slowly and he can hear the sound of Christmas music playing faintly.

"It's that time of year again," he recalls. "A lot of people look forward to it. I try to, but it's not as easy to find happiness in this season as it once was".

For him, it's a time of reflection. A time to think about all the stupid mistakes he has made over the past year, and where he went wrong and what he can do differently to make things right. He's walking down the sidewalk, hood up, head down to the ground. Slowly the cracks in the sidewalk pass by through the fog of his breath. Each step brings him closer to his destination.

"I used to know why people were so happy during the holidays. I used to know what it felt like to wake up Christmas morning with a smile on my face. I used to understand what it meant to be with someone on Christmas and hold them in my arms as we cuddled up near the fireplace. Those days are long gone. In order to truly appreciate the holidays, you need to have someone to spend it with. Always wanted to get married, settle down, have a kid or two. Guess it just wasn't in the cards for me."

As he passes by a restaurant, he notices a couple holding hands through the window. "Everywhere I go, I'm reminded of what 'could have been' - the life I could've had. I've wasted so many opportunities. Nights like these remind me of just how cold my life is."

He comes to a crosswalk and pauses, waiting for the light to change. He glances over at a car stopped at the light. In the car there's a little girl holding a teddy bear. Her eyes are filled with joy. She looks right at the man as if she feels sorry for him. "Why's she looking at me like that, like I'm some old wretch that needs help?" he wonders.

The light changes. The man takes a step forward and notices out of the corner of his eye that the girl's eyes are still fixated on him as the car she's in drives away. "I remember being that age once. I also remember staring at people that looked different than me. I suppose a man with a long beard and ragged clothing doesn't quite fit society's depiction of "normal." "Guess I can't blame her for staring at me like that. Children are so honest - a lot more honest than any adult you'll ever meet. You can always count on their eyes to tell you the truth. They always seem to see you for who you really are."

There was a time when this man would have felt sorry for himself after noticing someone looking at him like that. But not anymore. He's given up on feeling sorry for himself. He gave up long ago. His destination is just ahead. The stars are shining faintly through the heavy clouds above. But this is no night for stargazing. Not for this man. It's getting colder. "There's the old bridge. I've finally arrived. I have a lot of memories at this old bridge." He used to come up here with his dad when he was a kid, and they'd watch the old train pass below them. He even had his first kiss here. Molly Winters, sixth grade. "That was one for the books, "he recalls. "I'll never forget it." "Where has time gone, anyway? Look at me. Look at these hands. I never thought I'd see the day when my hands would turn to prunes. And my face, covered in these shaggy whiskers. Guess that ol' dapper charm has worn off." "Sure is getting cold out here. Seems like it's dropped ten degrees since I started." "Well, no need to stand around any longer. Came here for a reason, after all."

He takes a deep breath and looks down at the train tracks below. He forces a smile on his face, closes his eyes, and jumps... Snow begins to fall silently. The wind dies. A beautiful calm fills the air. Somewhere across town, a little girl sits by her bedroom window, holding her teddy bear. She watches the snowflakes fall slowly. A tear rolls down her cheek as the sound of sirens roars in the distance.

Calamus Gladio Fortior

Some people speak volumes with thundering vocals, others make their message loud and clear through protests, swinging their powerful messages through the air.

I speak softly and let my pen do the speaking.

Calamus Gladio Fortior: The pen is mightier than the sword.

Words cut deeper than the sharpest blades, thoughts suffocate like airborne poisons, conviction wraps tightly around lost souls like unbreakable chains.

I refuse to become what the world tells me I should be, refuse to walk the path of the arrogant, the ignorant or the blind.

I have a voice, and it will be heard.

I fight my battles with words created by carefully crafted thoughts, banging inside your mind to the rhythm of my own beating heart.

I create strokes of compassion, rip out the pages of anger and apathy and expose them for all the world to see. I shed light on the ink stains that saturate the guilty and cover up the sins of those sitting comfortably in their high towers.

With each letter of every word I'll pour my heart and soul into an ocean, each day growing larger and larger, until one day it's waves of truth and love will spill out and engulf the entire world, awakening them from their slumber and filling their hearts and minds with new thoughts and ideas to rebuild what's left of the empire once built with our flawed human hands.

My pen will tear apart the veil like a dagger ripping down one's chest, exposing the darkened hearts of those who have danced with the demons, indulged in libations of their own bodily fluids, and climbed their way into moist caverns to spread their disease. The demons won't be able to hide when my words cut down their hideaways, ripping them to shreds as they crawl away in agony.

I see things no one else can see, hear words unspoken, feel emotions from other dimensions.

I am the thinker, the one who ponders, the dreamer.

These thoughts won't ever go away. Strike me down and throw my corpse into the ocean and my ideas will flow through the deepest depths, saturating the very source of life itself, pierce my flesh with bullets and my blood will spill onto the ground and guide you home, rip my brain from my skull and these thoughts will be released into the cosmos, eternally skipping off the stars until reaching some faraway hearts and minds.

Don't tell me who you think I should be. Don't try to change me.

The most dangerous wars are fought not with guns and knives, but with ideas, with thoughts, with carefully crafted words of mass destruction.

I have that power.

Love me.

Hate me.

Fear me.

But never doubt me.

Never doubt the power of the words inside my mind, the deep love for humanity inside my heart.

With this pen I'll wage war, tear down the walls, bring the demons to their knees, free the captives, drown the arrogant in their own tears, bring hope to the hopeless, expose the rapists, the sexist pigs, and the self-righteous assholes. With a humble heart and a sharpened quill I will bring light to the darkness of false religion, snuff out racism and bring liberation and hope to every color, every belief and every gender.

I dare you to stop me, dare you to rip this pen from between my fingers.

No words will be left unspoken. No stories left to be told.

I am the writer, the hero of my own story. My words are eternal. I will never be silenced.

Calamus Gladio Fortior.

"Look at us, fractions of our former selves. Can we find love in this wasteland? Can we survive on used hearts that don't beat as strongly as they used to?" – The Ghosts

In Sickness and in Death

I don't know how much time we have left. The future has never felt so uncertain. So I'll hold you just a little tighter tonight. I'll love you a little deeper, kiss you a little longer.

These times are uncertain, but I promise you my love for you will never die.

From inside our small fortress we gaze out into the world outside. It seems so peaceful out there tonight.

But death is surely out there, working around the clock to deliver his choking touch.

In the still night air he sweeps across the neighborhoods, swiping his long scythe across our friends and families, our lovers, our childhood heroes, those we hold so dear in our hearts.

How many more will die tonight?

How many innocent children will never wake up to another summer day? How many lovers will wake up with an empty spot in their bed where love once resided?

It's so quiet out there. Too quiet.

And yet somewhere in the distance the constant beeping of respirators pump oxygen all through the night, while nurses run towards lungs gasping for breath, using every last ounce of energy they have left, desperately trying to save them.

If you listen carefully enough you can hear them crying into their pillows at night, asking God why they couldn't save them, why little Amy had to take her last breath tonight, why James couldn't say goodbye to his wife before he slipped away with tears streaming down his face, why Olivia had to die knowing that she was taking her baby with her and there was nothing she could do to save the little one.

It's a senseless thing, this sickness. It doesn't judge, it doesn't stop and seems content with taking lives without a single thought of regret.

God help us, if we ever survive this will we ever make sense of it? Will we ever find comfort again? Will happiness return to our hearts?

Life has always been uncertain, and tomorrow has never been guaranteed for any of us. But death has never been so close to knocking on our door.

So I'll hold you more tightly in my arms tonight. When I kiss you goodnight I'll pause for a moment and gaze into your eyes and do my best to capture your beautiful face like a photograph in my memory. I will wake up in the middle of the night just to whisper "I love you" into your ear. I'll savor every moment with you as if it was our last.

And I'll pray with you that death will spare a few more tonight, that no more wives will have to go to bed alone, that no more children will wake up to find their mothers and fathers are gone, that no more tiny hearts cease to beat again.

And if you should wake up one day to find me gone, know that my love for you will reach beyond the grave and envelop you for all time, and that I'll be waiting for you on the other side. I waited a lifetime to find you, and I'd wait an eternity more for you.

One day our lungs will breathe again. One day our hearts will start beating once more. One day we won't take each other for granted any more. One day our love for each other will be stronger than it's ever been and humanity will continue, it will thrive, and we will begin again.

So death, put away your scythe. We're ready to start living.

Editor's note: If you or anyone you know is working in the medical field right now, please know that my prayers are with you. And please send anyone you know in the medical field right now a text or message telling them your thoughts or prayers are with them. And please thank them for the work they are doing and for risking their lives and their families' lives every day to try and save those affected by this terrible sickness. Let them know we care. And may God bless us all.

Memory

Yesterday you were smiling in the sunshine in a beautiful Technicolor world. Today you're just a black and white memory in fading photographs and grainy 8 millimeter films.

As time passes, your memory goes with it, and generations pass, never having the chance to feel your warm embrace or hear the sound of your echoing laughter that brought cheer to everyone around you.

Your jewelry, which you once wore so proud now sits scattered across pawn shops and in the drawers of distant relatives who don't remember your name.

Your once radiant clothes now sit at the bottom of a city dump, torn to shreds by earth's cruel elements.

Your body lies below, now one with the soil.

You have become a memory, a lifetime lived now just an eternal thought.

All those happy memories that you made, surely they still exist somewhere on the fabric of time, echoing softly through the years.

Wherever you are, can you still hear us? Do you still whisper in our ears and tell us how much you love us?

Time is the cruelest of things. Despite our best efforts we can't stop it. It is the juggernaut that pushes us forward. And time stops for no one.

But I wonder if time has stopped for you and those who have passed before. If so, how does it feel? With the burden of time lifted, is there more love to give? More life worth living? Or has every moment lost its meaning? Without time, what is a moment, but a fraction of eternity?

Wherever you are, wherever you've gone, your memory lives on in these black and white images that remind us of a time when lives were touched by your radiant presence. Does a smile keep brightening the lives of those who see it even after one has passed? Do pictures of a forgotten era contain little pieces of time worth revisiting?

We once said goodbye to you, but one day we will again say hello to that beautiful smile, in a place where time can't stop us, can't age us, and can't break us apart.

Ride With Me

"Kids just don't seem to do things with their grandpas these days."

That thought lingered on in my mind as I drove home one day in the pouring rain. I'd just left the hospital, where my grandpa had been lying in a lonely bed for two months after suffering a stroke.

He kept telling me how much he missed working in his garden. He and my grandma had been toiling away at it for more than 40 years.

The day that I visited him in the hospital, we talked about some of the adventures we used to have together when I was a kid.

It's been over 20 years now, but I can still remember the summer of 1992. In some ways, that summer shaped me into who I would become years later.

Life was much simpler back then, somehow the hours passed by much slower. Long summer days seemed to linger on for an eternity, and the three short months that we enjoyed out of school never seemed to end. It was a time of youthful energy, optimism and innocence. I didn't know what the future held back then, and I didn't really care. I didn't worry about tomorrow, didn't dwell on the past. Today was all that mattered, and what could be done to make it as special as possible.

I used to spend a lot of time at my grandparents' house as a child. Today it's hard for me to imagine having the time to spend all day there and then still have enough hours left in the day to play with my friends when I got home.

But grandma and grandpa's house was a special place. And my grandpa was a special person.

I swear, I never saw him blow his top once, never heard him yell at anyone or tear someone down. He was the kindest person I ever knew. And he wasn't just my grandpa, he was more like a friend, a special kind of friend that you could reminisce about the old times with, ask what it was like to live in a world that was "completely in black and white," and learn really cheesy jokes from.

I had a lot of friends back then. I did all the things normal kids did. Not a day went by when one or two of my friends weren't banging on the front door asking if I could come out and play football with them or check out the newest video game to rent.

I don't know how many other kids my age hung out with their grandpas, but if they did, they never talked about it. I guess I felt pretty special to have the opportunity to hang out with him. A lot of kids my age seemed to look down on the elderly because they weren't "cool" enough. But grandpa was a pretty cool guy to me. I loved to hear tales of his adventures in Japan, where he was stationed during the Korean War, and the wild adventures that he and his buddies had. It was all very fascinating to a young boy like me, who hadn't truly "lived" yet.

One thing we used to do is ride bicycles together all over town, and in the summer of '92, we were riding in style. I was the talk of the neighborhood with my neon green and blue Huffy, and grandpa, well, he was sporting a classic 1950's-style cherry-red bicycle that he meticulously painted himself, complete with adjustable mirror.

We were born to be wild on our bikes, and where we were going, we didn't need roads.

The sky was the limit on our bicycle adventures, and many times we narrowly escaped with our lives from evil sorcerers, savage beasts and even the seedy "dark territory" underworld of the oil refinery.

I'm sure most people thought we looked pretty silly riding all over town together, but I didn't care at all. I was having the time of my life.

I remember one day in particular, one that I'll never forget. We'd been riding for about 2 hours, and grandpa decided we should stop and sit on the curb to rest for a bit. We started out with small talk, with stories of grandpa's childhood and what he remembered about World War II. But then the subject of God came up somehow. Grandpa started talking about the one person that has carried him through his life, the one constant that's kept him out of trouble – Jesus. Grandpa then started tearing up, as he always did when he talked about Jesus. He told me, "Corey, if there's one thing I want you to learn from me before I leave this world, it's this: Jesus loves you, and He'll always be there for you."

Initially I didn't know how to respond. I just sat there in silence. And then tears started rolling down my cheeks.

That moment had such an impact on my life that I have remembered it all these years. And because I respected my grandpa so much, I took those words to heart, and have carried them with me ever since.

There, on a hot sunny day in 1992, two people from completely different generations shared a moment together that would last a lifetime.

After a moment of silence, grandpa and I got up and mounted our bicycles and continued on our journey.

As I get older, a lot of things I've experienced in the past start to make more sense. Little things that might not have seemed like much at the time suddenly become clear to me, and I often find myself reflecting on those little moments, and becoming inspired by them.

I suppose that getting older at least brings that advantage. For all the things that go wrong in our lives, the endless worries that come, the heartaches and pain both inside and out, there is still comfort in looking back on those special moments.

That's what keeps me going some days. As dark as things seem to get sometimes, or as hopeless as it seems, I hold on to those happy memories, so that I can smile again.

As I look back on my life, it's not the big things that have changed me. It's the small things. I've found that God is a master of subtlety, sneaking in life's little lessons into the seemingly mundane parts of life.

Grandpa unfortunately passed away eight years ago, but not before we had one more time to reminisce about the "good old days."

One day, not long before he passed away, he asked me if I remembered the good times we had riding bikes together.

I told him it was the best time of my life.

"You remember that day we sat on the curb, and I told you about Jesus?" he asked.

I told him I could never forget that day.

He just looked at me with a smile, put his hand on my shoulder and said "That was a good day, Corey. I'll never forget it either."

I will never forget my grandpa, Robert Kneedler, and the great times we had together. And I look forward to the day that he and I will be reunited in heaven so that we can continue our bicycle riding adventures together.

And I owe it to grandpa to be the best man I can be, and to spend the rest of my days making meaningful memories with my loved ones.

I could never be a fraction of the man my grandpa was, but I know he's up there somewhere, looking down on me with love. And that thought will carry me through the darkest nights ahead.

Thank you, Grandpa, if you can somehow read this. Thank you for everything. And keep that bicycle in tip-top shape, because someday soon, we're going to ride again.

Legacy

How many times will I rip my heart out of my chest before it stops beating?

How many miles will I travel before my legs stop moving?

How many tears before this well runs dry?

How much anger before it turns into hatred?

How many promises broken before I quit trusting?

How much weight before my body breaks down?

How many seasons before change happens?

How much suffering before going numb?

How many sacrifices before there's nothing left to give?

There is only one answer to these questions:

Madness.

Picture Perfect, Part 2

You're sitting there next to him with his arm around you in the sanctuary, but he feels like a total stranger to you.

This man is your husband, the man you swore yourself to at the holy altar before both God and man seven years ago.

And now he's staring across the room at another woman while the pastor preaches a message about faithfulness.

You know what he's probably thinking. He's undressing that polka dot button-up top in his mind, imagining where his hands would go if he could just get her alone with him.

And then he puts his hand on your thigh. You want to scream, but you can't. You want to cry, but you don't want to make a scene, afraid of what he might do to you later.

He winks at you, like it's all some kind of sick joke. How are you supposed to respond to that? He expects you to just sit there and take it like a "good little housewife."

It takes every lay ounce of energy to force a smile on your face, knowing that if you don't, there could be consequences.

You swear you hear the pastor mention something about slavery in his sermon. That's what you feel like: a slave to this self-righteous boy trapped in a man's body.

He's a man of God, all right. Exactly the man you thought he was when you tied the knot.

At least that's what everyone else seems to think.

By all appearances he certainly seems to be.

He's fooled them all, hasn't he? The charming smile, that firm hand-shake, that overpowering masculinity and the pleasant scent of his expensive cologne.

He shakes hands with the same hand he uses to slap you in the face when he gets drunk, uses that same grin when he stands naked in the doorway like some kind of sick psychopath, ready to force his dick inside you, whether you want it or not.

"Wives, submit to your husbands."

How many times has he mumbled that verse during his drunken rages? How many times has he preached the good word in the bedroom while he digs his fingernails into your back and pulls your hair back until your neck feels like it's going to snap?

Church is nothing more than a social club for him, a way to mingle with his holy buddies and show off his trophy wife.

God should probably damn him, but somehow he slithers in like a snake every Sunday morning and injects his poisonous words into everyone he speaks to.

And yet, the hour and a half spent in this holy place is the only respite you get from the hell of living with this man every day.

When Sam comes up to you and shakes your hand like a true gentleman, you want to scream "TAKE ME!" but you know you could never escape. Besides, you don't think you would ever deserve a man like him. You can see in his eyes that he cares. He gives you that look that no one has ever given you before - that look of adoration, of compassion, of sincere empathy - looks that your husband has never thought of giving you.

Lust.

That's the only look you ever see in his eyes, but only when he feels like it. And if the dirty magazines don't satisfy his desires, then he'll use your body as a warm vagina to fantasize about a woman stuck to a two-dimensional piece of paper.

This is the man of God who has everybody fooled.

But how many others are here too?

When you look around the room, suddenly you notice the solemn look on the faces of other women. Could they be just as miserable as you are? The thought terrifies you.

But it's probably true, you figure. The majority of their smiles are masks they wear to cover up their fear, their shame, their regret.

You realize you're not alone, and for a moment that's the only ounce of peace you feel inside. But you know it won't last for long. When the church bells ring and it's time to leave, you'll all have to go back to your miserable lives, and the cycle will repeat over and over down every block, as it has for so many generations.

When you walk out with the kids, he will stay behind as he always does, mingling with other men, sharing conversation about who has a bigger boat, then he'll move on to the attractive women and make the rounds with them while you and your children are sitting in the hot car burning up.

You'd argue with him for taking so long, but you learned a long time ago that was another trigger for him, so you keep your mouth shut. The kids are too young to understand, so they suffer for reasons unknown to them.

"What's taking daddy so long, mom? He always does this."

You never know which answer to give them.

When he gets in the car you see a piece of paper hanging out of his pocket. Probably someone's phone number. Your first thought is that it's another woman's number, but you convince yourself it's probably from one of his golfing friends.

He's always happy on the car ride back home. Why is he always so happy? Probably because his ego is filled to the brim. Lord knows he's not going to church to worship anyone but himself.

"What's wrong with you? Smile, baby!" He says as he puts his hand again on your thigh, then slowly starts sliding it toward your crotch.

"Scott! The kids are in the back seat!"

But he doesn't care.

He's going to get it one way or another.

As the car speeds down Fourteenth Street, drivers are completely unaware of the chaos that erupts inside the blue Nissan Murano that Scott and Victoria Maples and their two small children are traveling in.

Minutes later, drivers could see smoke coming from the ditch by Glendale Hills, a newly built housing district consisting of cookie cutter homes that all look alike.

It doesn't take long for the sirens to go off and an ambulance and fire truck deployed to the scene.

Victoria finally got her wish. She found her escape from the American hell she'd been trapped in.

Too bad she won't live to see it through.

Authorities arrive on the scene and find Scott with a broken nose. In the back seat the kids are shaken up, but they'll be ok.

"I don't know what happened, officer. My..head suddenly started spinning.."

The officer accepts his lie. Scott doesn't even think for a moment about his dead wife slumped over in her seat next to him.

Scott would get his way. One month later he'd be getting it on with Kelly, the woman he'd exchanged phone numbers with at church while the kids sat on the living room floor watching SpongeBob, neglected and hungry.

A beautiful feminine flame was extinguished on that fateful day, and another chapter closed in the book of American dreams.

"Maybe I wasn't so artificial after all.
Maybe I was more human than I realized.
Maybe I wasn't the person I thought
the world despised." — The Ghosts

Doctor's Note

Dear Mr. Nelson,

It has come to my attention that you have, as of late, been staggering around like a mindless zombie, unsure of what direction to take.

This is not uncommon, given your recent circumstances, but I think we can remedy this condition.

Here's what we're going to do, Mr. Nelson. You know all those memories you have locked up inside your head of things that you think are significant? Things that mean something to you? Well, we're going to remove them. Now, I know this is probably going to be hard for you, but I assure you, you'll be better off without them. We're going to make a brand new man out of you, Mr. Nelson. And you're going to thank us when it's all over.

The procedure doesn't take long, and believe it or not, you might actually enjoy it.

I know you've always tried to avoid the "pleasures" of this world, but I assure you that for this procedure, you're going to have to let loose a little bit.

The first thing you need to do, Mr. Nelson, is let go of those silly morals you've held onto for all these years. That's right, you don't need them. Where have they gotten you all these years, anyway? And when you come into my office, I don't want to hear anything about how "important" it is to be the "good guy," and how taking the straight and narrow path leads to true happiness.

No Mr. Nelson, there's simply no time for preaching now, and quite frankly, I just don't want to hear it. You've got to get back on your feet so you can start living! Once we've taken those pesky morals out of you, we're going to need your mind. Oh, don't worry, we're not going to take the whole thing away from you, just the parts that make you.. "feel."

We can't have feelings getting in the way of pleasure now, can we?

Once we have your mind, we're going to strip the skin from your body.

There's no reason to hang on to that old bag that you were born with. No one's ever really happy with their own skin, are they? Of course they aren't. So we're going to take that away from you as well. Think of it as a.."rebranding."

Don't worry, we won't leave you walking around as a skeleton. We're going to give you brand new skin Mr. Nelson, and the best part is, we'll leave our signatures on it so you'll never forget this very important procedure that changed your life. I know that you are no doubt sweating out the details right now as you read them, but I assure you, this is the path that you'll want to take. Oh, and I almost forgot to mention. You'll need to take a few medications to help you along after the procedure, just to make things more..enjoyable for you. These come in various forms such as glass bottles, cans, pills, little plastic bags, and the occasional needle. Nothing you can't handle, right?

Think about it. A brand new you that everyone will love, a body that women will truly desire and no pesky mind or morals to get in the way of having a good time! Trust me, I'm a doctor. Would I ever steer you in the wrong direction? Of course not. The entire world can be yours, Mr. Nelson. All you need to do is change everything about yourself. It's that simple. And the best part is, you're going to have the time of your life.

I look forward to seeing you in my office on Friday.

Sincerely,

Dr. Nicholas Apollyon

Child

All I can do is hide this child inside me, hide my insecurities, hide my fears. Cover up the confusion, hold back the tears.

The world will see a grown-up shell, but deep inside I'll reside in this childhood hell.

My body has grown but my mind never truly developed.

My brain stopped growing after the depression crept in and it was enveloped.

I cry out into the night like a newborn when no one can hear.

I cry out for someone to save me, but help is never near.

I am fragile and weak, but I conceal it each day behind this beautiful physique.

I want to scream at the top of my lungs, but the adult world says "No, we can't expose our feelings so we should all hold our tongues."

So I'll continue to hide behind this facade, pretend like I have it all together and earn their applause.

I'll strut into the office and pretend that I'm an adult, and prove to my boss that I can produce acceptable results.

If the world is a nursery then I'll make this my playpen. And I'll relive this childhood hell over and over again.

Clover

I hate you today, but if you ever went away I'd never see the light of another day.

Isn't it sad that it takes a lover's passing to realize how much they meant to you?

It's so tragic that death is so often the catalyst that brings life and love into view.

I don't want to wake up one day and realize I'll never see you lying next to me with that beautiful smile.

Please promise me you'll stay awhile.

I'm sorry my heart is in so much pain, sorry my world is drenched in the cold rain.

I promise you that no matter the weather, whatever the disaster, I'll love you all the same.

Even when it seems impossible to go on, I'll keep choosing you every day, from the cold of winter to the warmth of May.

Just promise me you won't go away. Promise me I'll never have to lay flowers down at another lonely grave.

You are the one I could never get over, my lucky four-leaf clover.

Sober

I write songs without music. Lyrics without the companion of a guitar or the pounding, steady beat of a drum. Words with meaning pour out of my mind like a waterfall. While the world passes me by, I spin inside my own galaxy, observing from light years away, watching hope bloom with each new day, listening to arguments, collecting the broken dreams of the weary. I take it all in, try my best to process it all, and create beautiful portraits from those dreams and disasters of everyday life.

My choices led me here to this lonely place. But that doesn't mean I can't make the most of it while I'm here.

Every man must eventually face his own mortality. My life has slowed to a crawl as everyone else moves at a steady pace, blissfully unaware of what's ahead for them.

When you're alone in the stars, all you have is your thoughts to keep you company. I stopped questioning why I got here a long time ago. The anger toward myself, toward others - it faded away years ago.

The key? Accepting that ultimately, all that anyone really cares about is themselves. With no air to breathe out here, my lungs have filled with apathy.

I've accepted my lonely fate here among the stars. It's beautiful up here, you know.

Surrounded by such gorgeous sights, how could I ever want anything more? I've given my life to the vastness of space - the quiet, peaceful existence everyone spends their whole lives chasing after with money, fast cars, spouses, big houses and fancy church memberships.

Funny how meaningless it all seems from this perspective. You can't see it from down there, can you? No, I don't suppose you can. But one of these days, you will.

Time II

Four years old. Devon and I are sitting on the couch watching "David the Gnome." Two characters rub noses in the show, a gesture of affection between the gnomes. Devon looks over at me and smiles, then leans in to rub her nose against mine. We both giggle uncontrollably.

Six years old. Christina and I are on the playground at school. She pulls me behind one of the bushes next to Mrs. Andrews' class. I gaze into her eyes with a look of bewilderment, but anxious excitement fills my heart. She closes her eyes and puckers her lips. I take a deep breath and kiss her quickly on the lips. Her face turns red as she smiles. "Is this...love?"

Eight years old. Valentine's Day. I'm sitting in Mrs. Sweeten's class. Across the room, Ashley pulls out a crayon from her 64-pack box. She then writes something on a valentine, then looks at me winks. She then passes it to two classmates in between us, and when it reaches my desk, my heart is beating quickly. I unfold the heart-stamped paper and the words "I love you" are staring back at me.

10 years old. Jennie and I have been hanging out all summer. We've been on many adventures the last three months, but the highlight of those 90 days is when we're lying on a blanket in my front yard holding hands. "Do you think we'll ever see each other again?" She asks me with tears streaming down her face. She and her family were moving to Colorado when summer ended. "I...hope so," I told her, just barely able to hold back the tears myself.

12 years old. Sara is so beautiful. I can't take my eyes off her. I've been daydreaming again, picturing us kissing, holding hands, walking down the beach together. "But she'll never be mine," I think to myself. The next day I walk to our classroom and she's waiting outside the door for me. "Hey handsome," she says with a smile. My heart skips a beat.

16 years old. Kelly and I are making out in her grandma's garden shed. My hands slowly move from her neck and onto her chest. Uncontrollable passion fills the tiny space and we can't keep our lips from touching. She slowly moves her hand downward. "Kelly? Are you in there?" It's her grandma. We panic.

18 years old. Jennifer shows up on my front porch holding the necklace I gave her with my senior ring attached to it. We'd just broken up the night before. "I just...wanted to return this."

I'm still angry with her for spending time with Rick, so I aggressively rip it from her hands and slam the front door. We never speak again. She would try to call a couple times but the damage had already been done. I was finished with her.

22 years old. I'm supposed to be studying, but I don't care because we are so lost in the moment. Our clothes piled up on the floor next to us, and we're trying to keep quiet so the neighbor doesn't hear us. Suddenly I hear a knock on the door. Before I could look up, she grabs my hair and pulls my head back to her face. "Shh." We resume our midafternoon delight. Outside, the College Christian singles group is waiting for me to answer the door. I'd promised them I'd go to a movie with them a couple days ago.

23 years old. We just had a fight, and I'm fuming. I'm tired of being stuck with her. She won't ever leave. I'm tired of her laziness, tired of her

mood swings. I tell her to get out of my apartment. Later that afternoon I drove to the river and took off my promise ring and threw it into the river. "I don't need you. I don't need anyone!"

25 years old. We've been at it all day, sinning between the sheets for hours, stopping only to eat a quick meal and then continue into the evening hours until we can't move any more. I look over at her lying next to me. She's so hot. I'd do it again if she'd let me. But something in my mind tells me this is it. That there's not going to be anything else but this. I feel an emptiness inside my heart, but I ignore it because my passion takes over.

26 years old. We've been married for a little over a year, and I find out she's been cheating on me. She's hiding her addictions behind my back, but the money is going somewhere and it's certainly not going to bills. I stumble into the kitchen and nearly trip over an empty bottle of her NyQuil. The kids are hungry. I'm hungry. I'm sick. Sick of her lies, sick of her unfaithfulness, sick of living with someone I hate, sharing this horrible nightmare she's created.

29 years old. I'm finally free. God help me, I finally escaped from that hell. Somehow, I made it to the other side, and I still feel an overwhelming guilt inside my gut. Did I do the right thing? Could I have saved it? I tried. But there wasn't anything left to save. The kids are okay. They're the only ones who matter. I think everything is going to be okay.

31 years old. It feels weird to date again, but Rachel and I are looking into each other's eyes and she makes me feel happy again. She tells me I'm the most amazing guy she's ever met. That I have a heart of gold. After sharing a heart to heart, she tells me she can't believe someone would ever take advantage of someone as kind as me. Two months later, she breaks up with me because she says she doesn't know how to handle

a "nice guy." She tells me I'm too good for her and she walks away. I'm left completely confused by this.

32 years old. I've been dating a beautiful blonde woman for a couple months. It started out beautifully. But it doesn't matter what I say or do now- I'm living in the shadow of her ex-husband. He was horrible to her. Emotionally abused her for years. She claims to suffer from PTSD. I tell her I'll do one thing and she twists it into something her ex would do before I have a chance to act. She turns me into a bad guy I've never been, nor could I ever be. The next day before she ghosts me and blocks me, she says, "We aren't compatible. I don't ever want to see you or hear from you ever again."

34 years old. Cold night in December. Ghosted again. She left with no explanation. No goodbye. No conflict, no problems, just disappeared. I played all my cards right, did everything right. I was always myself, kind and gentle. Always understanding. They come and go. Tell me I'm the "Most Amazing" guy they've ever met. Not like the others. Handsome. In touch with my own feelings. Respectful, a real gentleman. And then they suddenly disappear with no explanation. I've had enough. The straw has finally broken the camel's back. Frustrated as hell, my mind fills up with anger. What the FUCK is wrong with people these days? What ever happened to logic? Whatever happened to the common courtesy of saying goodbye? Every day feels like waking up to the same day over and over again. Feels like nothing's ever going to change. I've had enough. I'm tired of chasing after something I truly believe now that I'll never have. It's time to hang up my hat, time to walk away from this aimless endeavor.

God, whatever happened to logic? Whatever happened to true love? It's like I woke up one day, and the world suddenly stopped making sense.

Five years old. I wake up in my bed to the sound of my mom's voice.
"Corey, it's time to wake up. Come downstairs for breakfast!"

I wipe the sand out of my eyes and slowly rise, grabbing my favorite
teddy bear before heading down the stairs. My mom sits down a bowl
of Lucky Charms onto the table for me. "Do you want milk or orange
juice?" She asks me. "Milk is fine," I tell her. My dad walks into the room
in his work suit holding a briefcase. "Hey kiddo, did you sleep well?"
He then walks to my mom and gives her a kiss goodbye. "I'll see you in
a few hours, honey." They both smile at each other and wave goodbye.
Dad walks out the door and I look over to my mom and ask her, "Will I
ever be married someday like you guys? Will I be happy like that when
I'm with them?" She smiles at me and says, "Of course you will, honey.
That's what all boys do. They grow up and find the love of their life and
get married and live happily ever after."

"But mom, what if...I don't get that?"

"Of course you will, honey. You're a good boy. You deserve the most
wonderful girl this world has to offer!"

34 years old. I'm cold. I'm tired.

I finish saying a prayer with my son and tuck him

Into bed. "Good night, buddy. I love you." I shut his door gently and
for a moment, I feel a sense of sadness pour over me. "I wonder if I'll
ever find someone," I think. "I wonder if she's even out there at all." My
heart sinks down into my chest, thinking he might never know the true
gentle touch of motherly love, never wake up to see his dad kiss his wife
goodbye before heading off to work.

But then I realize that "even if it's just you and me, buddy, that's enough.
Because you make me happier than anyone in this universe ever could."
And I make a promise to myself that I will always be the best man I can
possibly be, not for a potential future wife, but for him. Because he is
my world, and that's all that really matters. And this love we have for

one another will be stronger than anything I could possibly find in this universe.

All of us are destined to love. Some are destined to love their neighbors, some to love their spouse, and some to love their sons and daughters. I consider myself blessed to love someone now, and to feel love back each and every day. That's all that really matters to me in this life.

Sure, things didn't turn out the way I'd planned. But plans rarely do.

I'm one of the lucky ones, I figure. So many out there have been trapped in horrible relationships, abused, neglected, taken advantage of. But here I am, not broken. Wiser and stronger than I've ever been before. And whatever lies ahead on this path of life, I know I don't have to walk it alone.

"Can I hold your hand, dad?"

"Of course you can, buddy."

"Where are we going?"

"I don't know, son. But whatever is ahead, it's going to be beautiful. And we're going to see it all together."

"That sounds like a good plan to me, dad. Let's go!"

Alive

I'm alive, and you are dead. And I wonder to myself, "who is better off?"
How could I have known that one day I'd wake up alone? How could I
have known our love would be cut short at such a young age?

If only I'd known.

All it took was one cough.

And then mine followed.

If only we'd known.

We were both sick. The coughing got worse. The fever ticked upward
each passing day. The air felt thinner with each laborious, wheez-
ing breath.

But then things seemed better. I felt better. You felt better. For a
moment, we could see the light at the end of this nightmarish tunnel.
So we went to bed that night, and as you blew me a kiss from six feet
away, you promised me a brighter future ahead.

But then you woke up in the middle of the night and spoke your final
words to me.

"It's okay, babe...I'll be okay," and your feverish body collapsed onto
the bedroom floor.

I can still hear the sound of sirens echoing in my mind as I held you on
the floor until the paramedics arrived.

And as I helplessly watched the blue hazmat suits wheel you away in
that orange body bag, so too went with you our dreams of a future with
a beautiful family and a white picket fence.

This invisible enemy, it doesn't care whose lives it takes. It spreads like
wildfire, ripping out hearts and leaving families torn in its path.

Why you? Why not me?

Was it merely stupid fate that took your breath away and left me alive with nothing but a broken heart? Or was it the miniscule difference in our genetics that handed me the better luck of the draw?

I have no answer.

No one can give me answers.

All I can do is cry. All I can do is pound my fists into the wall over and over again, hoping to God that somehow it will bring you back.

It's not fair. It's not fair that you had to go and leave me here holding what's left of my freshly broken heart in my hands.
We never asked for this. We never committed any crime to deserve this.
You were the greatest man I've ever known.
You still are.
You were my everything!
I can't stop thinking of that night I said my final goodbye to you.
I couldn't even touch you! Couldn't even kiss you goodbye!

I would have stopped the world, just to look into those beautiful brown eyes again and tell you that I love you.

I want to feel you right now, but I can't. I want to know that you're wrapping your arms around me but why can't I feel anything?
No goodbye. No whispering "I love you" into your ear.
And when I hit the floor I didn't want to get up. I wanted to die right there.
"Take me with you! Take me with you!" I screamed as loudly as I could.
It's not fair. None of it is fair.

Why, God? Why did this happen?

Give me a sign that you're there. Let me feel you again. Just one touch, just one breath.

It's hell without you. I can't go on like this.

Why can't I feel you? God, why can't I feel you?

It was too early for Luis and Sarah to be separated. Too early for their book to end.

And yet stories like this one repeat over and over every day. What will it take to stop it? How much longer will lives be torn apart?

For Sarah, all that's left is a memory. A memory of a man she loved with all her heart.

When someone you love becomes a memory, that memory becomes a treasure. A treasure that never loses its value.

Cherish those treasures with all your heart. There may not be much time left.

Connection

Hello.

I just wanted to tell you that I still care.

I know it's been a long time.

What's wrong?

Can't you hear me?

Maybe my signal isn't as strong as it could be.

Quiet, now. Listen carefully.

What? The dial appears to be broken.

Wait, don't go. Just give me a second to…

…………

………

……

Transmission lost.

Christmas Walk, Part 2

I step outside for a moment to enjoy the night air. It's a cold night. Snowflakes fall silently to the ground. I hear sirens in the distance. On nights like this, sirens can only mean one thing. The Christmas spirits have taken another life.

It's that time of year again. That wonderful time of year when suicide rates are up, alcoholics run rampant, and relationships fall apart all over this fine city.

'Tis the season to be jolly.

Phones vibrating. Must be the station. Seems like they're always short-handed on nights like these.

"Hello? Yeah.. I'll be right there."

Another suicide. Male, presumably late 50's. Jumped off a bridge. That'll leave a mess. It's a good 40 feet or so down to the tracks. Better let the wife know I'm leaving.

Oh wait, she's asleep. Better not wake her. I won't be long anyway. Emily's tucked in too. They'll be all right.

I'm getting into my car. It's cold. I hate starting cars up in winter. Stupid thing never wants to start right, either.

I turn the key.

It started right up. That's rare. Especially on a night like this, where everything seems to go wrong.

It's such a beautiful, quiet night. But you don't expect anything to go right on a night like this when you're in law enforcement. I can almost smell death in the air.

Snowflakes can't cover up the dark canvas painted with blood that this world has been steeped in for so long. Every time it snows you can still see the filthiness of the world poking through. All it takes is a closer look - no matter how beautiful it may seem.

I've arrived at my destination. I remember this bridge well. I've got a lot of memories here. My friends and I used to smoke under the bridge after class. Until Jonathan's dad caught us. He worked for the railroad. I miss being young and stupid sometimes. No worries back then.

No bodies splattered all over the pavement.

I'm getting out of my car. Guess I'll leave it running. Shouldn't take too long.

I'm looking down at the man's body. Everyone's silent. Snowflakes are falling, partially covering up his face. His head is split open. Blood is running down into the gravel between the tracks.

As many suicides as I've seen, you'd think I'd be used to it by now.

Every time I see another lifeless body ended senselessly like this, I can't help but ask "Why?"

Who was this man? Why did he do it? Why does anyone do it? Granted, we've all been at the end of our ropes before. Heck, I've been there myself countless times. But what exactly does it take to put a man over the edge?

Did he have nothing left to live for? Where is his family? Did they not care?

Did he have any children? Surely a man's life is worth more than this. Surely this man's legacy is meant for more than this.

Now he'll be remembered as another nameless cadaver lying dead on the tracks.

There's something in the air tonight. Something different. This night's not like the others. I just can't put my finger on what it is.

Another life sacrificed to the Christmas spirits.

Meanwhile, a little girl slowly opens her eyes.

"Daddy?" she whispers.

She grabs her teddy bear and walks into the hall. Her parents' bedroom door is open. She silently enters the room.

"Mommy, where's Daddy?" she murmurs.

Her mother is awakened by the sound of her daughter's quiet voice.

"He must have been called out, honey. Did you hear the sirens earlier?" she asks.

"Yes. I did," the girl, replies, hugging her teddy bear tightly.

"Mommy, why do people have to die?" she asks.

Her mother replies, "Well, honey... because death completes us. Without death, we can never truly live."

The little girl looks down at her teddy bear and smiles.

Paranormal Chorus

You're a ghost to me.

That's all you'll ever be.

Why did I dance with you?

Why did the music even start?

What use is this broken heart?

My heartstrings are broken, there's no tune left to play.

No reason left to dance, no reason left to sway.

It all came crashing down like a chandelier,

Hope broken into pieces and replaced with fear.

We've fallen to our knees, this dance floor has become our disease.

Into the ground we will decay into ashes.

The October wind will sweep us into dead branches.

Like the leaves, our fall was planned from long ago. This death between us is inevitable, drifting silently like winter snow.

No bands will play our song, no voices will echo our passion, and whatever is left will be withered and ashen.

Now we are but ghosts in the atmosphere, here today but before long we will disappear.

The Teddy Bear

The teddy bear has lost his smile.

Yesterday you were brand new, ready to take on the world, feeling the warm embrace of love, sharing in laughter and making happy memories.

Now you're tucked away in a dark corner, while each new day brings more decay to your worn body. Stuffing bursting from every seam, half of your right ear gone, one eye sagging down- you're barely recognizable.

You sit there and listen to the sound of the others' laughter, wondering when it will once again be your turn to play.

But face it: you're a has-been. Your time has come and gone, poor bear. Remember the happy times. Drown in your memories, because that's all you have left.

You wish so desperately that you could cry, but your eyes remain dry no matter how hard you try.

Sure, there's always the chance that they'll come back to you, if only for nostalgia's sake. But you know in your little stuffed heart that your hour has passed for good.

The years will come and go, and with each passing minute you become less and less a memory and soon, not long from now, you will be forgotten.

How does it feel, poor bear? Do you ever sit and wonder why time has been so cruel to you, why they've gone and left you alone?

What could you have done differently? Could you have stopped the hands of fate from turning?

Hard to make sense of any of it, isn't it?

Ah, well, no sense thinking too hard about it. After all, you do have an eternity to think about it now. Surely in time you will find all the answers. Time. Something we all wish we had more of until it's all we have left.

Be careful, too much time and too much thought can drive one to insanity, you know.

Anyway, Good luck to you, poor bear. May you find some sort of meaning in your lonely existence.

Now, if you'll excuse me, I've a date with Miss Spider at the old tea table. If you aren't busy later, stop by. We're just over there in the corner next to that box of old Christmas decorations. I'll make sure the cobwebs are cleared before you arrive. Good day, poor bear!

Strip

Plug it in, let it sink in. Just another day, another client, another death again.

Virginity struck down like a nun kneeling at the altar, innocence chipped away like a pickaxe to fragile shale.

In the night air you can feel the demons brushing past your cheeks, hear them singing in the cries of the broken.

A few pennies for pleasure, a handful of pills to numb the pain.

If you're lucky you'll get high tonight. High enough to forget how low you've sunk.

When they look at you they don't see you. They only see another warm vagina to take advantage of on a cold night for their own pleasure, just another frail body to leave bruises on before they go back to their wives and kiss their children goodnight.

When was the last time someone saw you for who you are inside? How long has it been since someone cared about your feelings?

When was the last time someone wrapped their arms around you and held you while you cried?

Tell me why it's worth it. Give me one good reason for this path you walk.

Why can't you go back? Are you afraid? Are you afraid of what they'll see when you walk in that door? Afraid they'll judge you, disown you, see you as nothing more than a whore who lost her humanity years ago?

You were someone's little girl once. A daddy's little princess, a mother's angel, a miracle to this world that brought tears of joy to grandmothers, brought excitement to the widened eyes of your siblings.

Where did it all go? Why did you choose to run away from it all?

It's not too late.

You're still here. Still alive.

So take what strength you have left and turn around. Take that first step and leave behind the painful memories.

Sometimes to find the truth, we need to turn around.

Sometimes it's not the path forward, but the one behind that leads back home.

It's not too late.

There's still time to be that little girl again.

The Old Song and Dance

Our bodies connect but our hearts flounder inside our chests.

This cycle must be broken before it rips us to shreds.

If we could find an escape, we'd take it.

If the exit door opened up for us, we'd go our separate ways. But for now, we'll pretend. We'll fool ourselves into thinking that all of this still matters.

We'll make love and fake it. We'll smile at each other with thoughts of hate.

We'll play house like we're married, but live like roommates trapped in a small space with no escape.

We will wake up every morning and ask ourselves why we are still here, and wonder if there is a better life waiting for us out there.

We will fool our friends, our family, our coworkers into thinking we've got it all together. That we are one, inseparable until the very end.

And we'll continue onward. The process will repeat like a broken record full of broken love songs.

Until it kills us.

The Painter

I'm throwing jars of old tears away just to save myself from the pain of having said goodbye so many times.

How many opportunities have I squandered? How many hearts have I shattered on this path I've walked to satisfy my own longing?

I'm like a painter with infinite blank canvases. When one picture perfect love wasn't good enough, I threw it away and painted a new one.

"Maybe a little more darkness in the hair, maybe a freckle or two here."

But like a focused painter sitting in a musty attic, I was all alone, surrounded by broken pictures of potential love.

With my own tongue I spoke words of passion into their ears, held them tightly and promised them the world.

But was I promising them the world, or promising myself a prized possession?

If life were a blank canvas, mine would have layers of false dreams painted on it. Perhaps I was better off before I made that first brush stroke. Besides, the purity of white snow is more beautiful than the colors of madness.

There are no happy accidents in my world.

There is only intentional sorrow, shared with the ones I was supposed to love.

If only I could reverse time, erase the sinful strokes, dilute the poisonous hues, thin out the hatred, paint a beautiful sky to fly through.

But it's too late. I'm running out of paint. Running out of excuses, running out of time.

I think it's time to paint a new picture.

I'll cover the canvas with black paint, and just a few splashes of red.

My final masterpiece.

I'll call it "The End."

The painter picked up a bullet, and smiled.

Endless Night

As numerous as the stars in the sky, as vast as the endless ocean waves, as numerous as every single grain of sand in the desert, so too are the infinite words inside my heart that I could paint endless paintings of how my heart beats for you.

There aren't enough words to ever describe the beauty you possess, both inside and out.

There's a black hole where the world's compassion once existed. I can think of no one else who would fill that void so perfectly.

In the depths of twilight, I look up to you like the brightest star, burning brightly in the sky, a light that could ever die.

I know it feels like we're floating endlessly right now in the outer space of our minds, trying desperately to draw closer, but being blocked by fragments of our broken hearts.

Even comets can be broken up, but when they enter earth's gravitational pull they are reunited once again before burning into a burst of passion that lights up the atmosphere.

I hope and pray that one day these pieces will become whole, and the infinite universe of words inside me will pour out directly into your healed heart.

I may be from Mars and you might be from Venus, but our worlds collided when we decided to leave our comfortable atmospheres. An explosion took place when we met that rocked the cosmos, an Earth-shattering eruption of thoughts and feelings and ideas and laughter and tears.

No matter how this space dust settles, I'm thankful to have shared this moment in time with you.

Perhaps one day, like a star's bright light, future generations might see our story burning brightly in the night sky.

"We'll swim in a sea of hatred and lies that will take the rest of our lives to forget. Love means everything baby, so let's take another drink to celebrate." —The Ghosts

Awash

I am a product of yesterday, a ghost of the past, a character in a play on the world's stage that's been woefully miscast.

I am human, flesh and bone. I walk among you on the same paved roads that lead us all home.

But my path is a little rockier than the one you walk. It's easier to walk on a path that's been paved than one that's covered with jagged rocks.

For centuries we were treated like a disease, a blight on a society that considered themselves free.

America, the land of the brave. Home of the fancy blue suits, talking heads and politicians with one foot in the grave.

The greatest country ever created. Built with countless tears, hard work and the freedom to complain.

People in suburbia moan about the paint on their white picket fences being chipped; at least they didn't wind up with an empty bottle on a cold night lying in a muddy ditch.

The married complain about their spouses snoring; but do they know what the sound of rats scurrying about at night sounds like under rotting holes in the flooring?

The wealthy businessmen angrily slam down their phones in frustration onto their ornate cedar desks on floors so high, while below so many of us lie on our backs choking on our own blood as we pray for hope to come down from the sky.

Maybe we weren't born with a silver spoon in our hands. Maybe the skin we live in is a beautiful reflection of our ancestors who came from different lands.

Don't blame me for the lives that are taken every day. Don't point your finger at me for wanting to be noticed, wanting to be heard, praying that my people will finally matter to this world in some way.

Have you ever walked a single step in a color other than your own? Has it ever occurred to you that underneath we all have the same color of bones?

Because of your sick prejudice, the ball has been rolling for far too long and now there's no stopping this.

Who painted you the color of a god? What made you think you were the only person in this world who isn't flawed?

When I look at you I see a tangled forest of hate, overgrown with lies. There's no way out of your twisted view of reality, no exit signs, no golden gate.

So many just like me have been stricken down by your discrimination, hung from bridges, shot down like dogs for the sake of this great nation.

Did any of it satisfy that lust for power, that ravenous hunger to devour them as they held their loved ones and cowered?

Shoving them down into the mud, when you stabbed them, did it surprise you that you both shared the same color of blood?

The rain may wash away the evidence, but one day you and your loved ones will drown in the coming flood.

It was you who set the world spinning on this mad course. It was you who rode in on your high horse, swearing you had all the answers, claiming to be salvation's one true source.

Where we are headed I can not say, but regardless of our color, one day we'll all decay in the same way.

It's time for us to cut our senseless chatter and take the time to focus on this dark matter.

Time Worn

Time flows through me like a river, breaking down my body into an inevitable fractured state, a prison which houses my soul before it will one day ascend.

Flashes of my mortality blink into my mind like strikes of lightning, reminding me of the decay within.

Waves crash on the beaches of my mind, erasing my memories with each passing day.

Eventually there will be nothing left.

I am only a man. Only human.

Whatever dreams we had, whatever happy moments we shared will be lost forever.

So I'll cherish these days as best I can. Make the most of every moment, moving forward through the fog, hanging on to what's here before the waves take it away.

Horizon

I am bigger than all my problems.

I'll knock down all the walls before me, become the warrior I'm meant
to be.

I don't know what's ahead, but I'm getting there whether I'm alive
or dead.

These gray skies are dissipating, the horizon is rearranging.

I'm finally chasing after the person I've always wanted to be.

I'll keep moving forward through this swamp, even when it's so dark I
can no longer see.

And when I fall, thank heavens God is bigger than me.

Projection

Refocus the frame, rearrange, and set the stage.

Life used to be painted with beautiful colors bursting off the page. Now it's painted with darkness and rage.

Time seems to stand still after you've gone over the hill, spinning tires, starting out the window, paying endless bills.

My body is weak, fragile, and some days I can barely speak. But if my mind could travel somewhere far away from here, maybe I'd be content, maybe find my place in this world, find a love that is heaven-sent. Maybe such fantasy isn't so far away. Maybe if I think about it hard enough day after day, I'll sprout wings like a butterfly and fly far, far away.

Starving

By appearance's sake she's got everything, but those green eyes hide a personal hell she can't escape from.

Behind that smile she's gone, and sometimes she wonders if she's ever coming back.

Like a hollow ghost she sits in front of her vanity every night alone staring at her face, sometimes tracing with her fingers those anxiety lines that seem to multiply daily.

She wonders if others like her feel the same way, wonders if their American dream wasn't what it seemed.

Trapped under the weight of hungry souls begging for her attention, her time, and what little energy she has left, she feels like she's about to break.

She can't look at him without wanting to cry, without wanting to run.

Sometimes it feels like she's living with a stranger.

Those once-handsome features he had are now the things she hates looking at the most when she wakes up next to him every morning.

When he comes to bed late at night and she can smell her perfume, her stomach turns. She wants so badly to throw up but she doesn't want to deal with him yelling at her for overreacting.

She always heard physical abuse was the most painful, but no one ever told her the emotional abuse stings forever.

She's strong but these wounds are stronger.

The more she fights, the weaker she feels and the more intense the pain inside.

A human being can only take so much.

She loves her children but sometimes she looks at them with dread, and she hates herself for it.

Why does she feel this way about her own children? Has she gone so far down this hole that the darkness has enveloped her heart?

It's hard to force a smile when your heart is barely beating, hard to keep your chin up when the person who is supposed to love you most beats you down every day.

With every ounce of energy and strength she has left, she somehow carries on, pretending everything is ok because that's the American way.

And when no one else is around, she screams. Sometimes it feels good but sometimes she ends up on the floor in tears.

Once she was someone's princess, someone's pride and joy.

Now she'd give anything for just one minute of attention, for someone to hear her speak for just one moment.

She will hang on until she can't any longer, until the strength runs out and she takes her last breath.

Despite hope's flickering light being somewhere out there in this darkened abyss she calls home, she can't help but repeat daily that old familiar phrase:

"Not every story has a happy ending."

Mirage

That was us in the photographs, holding hands wasn't it?

Wasn't that us visiting the Grand Canyon? Aren't those our kids that are making goofy faces in front of the camera?

That's you and me on the stage in the sanctuary, looking into each other's eyes, right? You look so beautiful in that dress

And look! Look at the way I'm looking at you. See? That's how I felt about you! You could always see it in my eyes.

"What?"

"What are you saying?"

"That...that's not us?"

"Then...what happened to us?"

That was...that was supposed to be us. All those happy memories, those adventures, the marriage, the kids...

Remember? We'd sit and talk about it for hours. We had our whole future planned out. It was all on track.

We were...supposed to be happy, weren't we?

What happened? Where...

Where did it all go wrong?

"Oh God, where did it all go?"

"Where...where am I?"

"Oh God, where am I? Where are you?

What on earth happened?"

Insanity? Hardly. He spends the majority of his days sitting in his recliner in the corner of a cold, lifeless room. Once a day Kelly, a nurse's aide walks into his room and grabs an old photo album off a dusty shelf. In it are pictures of a family. A family that are all strangers to him, yet at the same time familiar.

Frank Aberdeen was never married. Never had children, and never visited the Grand Canyon. In all truth, Mr. Aberdeen didn't really do much in his 86 years of existence. Well, I guess it depends on what your definition of "doing something" is.

By all accounts, Mr. Aberdeen had it all. A fancy house, all the latest luxury cars, a huge pool outside with a view to breathtaking mountains.

The CEO of a Fortune 500 company, he made a lot of money and wasn't afraid to spend it. But he never took the time to love. Never took the time to build real relationships.

His life was a fast lane filled with reports and figures, dollar signs, fine cigars and fancy bottles of wine.

And he never looked back.

Then one day he woke up in a nursing home and wondered where it all went.

Now all the money in the world couldn't buy him the life he thought he never wanted, couldn't buy him a wife, a family, a legacy worth leaving behind.

Now he stares into black and white photographs brought in by the nurses to give him some modicum of peace. Some kind of hope that he can dream of.

It's not too late, you know.

Your life isn't over yet. You've probably got a few decades left ahead of you. So if you're reading this right now and you think life is all about money, success and fancy cars, you might want to think about the things that really matter.

What kind of legacy will you leave behind? Will you be remembered by a plaque on the wall of a cold hallway that's passed by every day by people who barely take notice? Or would you rather be remembered as someone who lived, someone who loved, someone who wasn't too busy chasing after worldly pleasures and empty successes to take time for what really matters?

Let go of it now. You still have time.

Shift your focus toward true happiness.

And when you leave this world one day, they'll remember you for the move you brought, the laughter you shared, and the hope you passed down to future generations.

I hope you realize this before it really is too late.

"Who can we trust if we can't trust ourselves? How can we live if life has no meaning? Over our shoulders we throw away the lessons, not looking back because our failures keep repeating." – The Ghosts

Before we wake

Remember the days when a few beeps and some static would turn us on to a brand new frontier?

We were so innocent back then, untouched by the blood-soaked hands of corporate greed, lust for our own selfish desires, or the emotional pull of seductive words.

When did we become slaves to the screen? How long ago did we sign our souls over to the digital powers that be?

These digital landscapes make perfect canvases to paint our hopes, our dreams, our fears on.

We want to present to the world a picture perfect vision of what we've become, but the happy little trees died a long time ago.

When it's all over, when all is said and done and the computers compute their last algorithms, what will we be left with?

Is purpose found between keystrokes? Is happiness accumulated in the number of likes we receive?

It's a currency we can't trade for a single minute more in these temporary lives we live.

What have we to gain if we lose a part of ourselves with every revealing post, every status update, every blatant cry for attention?

We are losing the ability to love, sacrificing friendship for selfish desires, becoming slaves to the internet gods.

Where once rose petals spread across the bed represented relentless passion, now pixelated hearts replace physical gestures of human love.

Digital walls contain no footholds. Imaginary graves drag our virtual personas deeper day by day. There is no escaping this pit we've sunken ourselves into, no cure for this hunger for acknowledgement.

It's a kind of funeral, isn't it? We've lost ourselves in this wasteland, and all that's left of us are traces of our digital footprints, left so long ago when dreams were still reality.

Now we live in a world where reality is a dream, hidden behind liquid crystal displays that project into our minds the most beautiful deceptions disguised by perfect human bodies with fake smiles.

Our screams and cries for help are filtered out through transistors that guide faded emotion into desktop recycle bins. Nevertheless we carry on through the forest of evolving technology, searching for meaning amongst bits and diodes.

We've forgotten what we were searching for.

Maybe all this time we were searching for ourselves, defining our self-worth by a quantity of upturned thumbs and little red hearts, comparing our outward shells to beautiful shades of melanin and almond beige smeared via filters across acne-saturated and scarred visages that are hidden in shame from the critical eyes of the world.

Don't let them see the real you. Don't let them see your hideous face. Hide the truth, embrace your newfound digital persona and knock them dead with orgasmic lies.

Swimming through comments collecting words of positivity while drowning in the negative, we exhaust our energy trying to stay afloat amidst our virtual reality.

And on and on this digital relapse continues, stretching down the infinite superhighway of broken dreams.

The day we connected to this World Wide Web of lies was the day humanity disconnected from what we once knew as reality.

Heart

Falling in love is the easiest thing to do if you open up your heart to someone.

This isn't another sad one, not another depressing look at reality, not a poem about love lost.

No, this one's about the joys of waking up in the middle of the night and seeing someone you love lying next to you.

This one is about getting home after a long day at work and having someone's arms to fall into and being held tightly until the stress melts away and that frown on your face is replaced with a smile.

What you're reading right now is about the joys of giving your heart to someone who gives you theirs in return, someone who loves you just as much as you love them, someone who wakes up every morning and looks at you in awe because you're the most beautiful woman he's ever seen, even without any makeup on, even with those dark circles under your eyes and your hair a complete mess.

How many restless souls lie awake in bed tonight, wondering if they're ever going to be happy again?

You have to sink before you can swim. You have to take a dive before you can spread your wings and fly.

Some go their whole lives thinking they've lost it, they've messed up and no one will ever want them again.

That's not true.

The only person telling you that is you. No one else.

You deserve to be held in the night by that special someone, deserve to come home to a candlelit dinner some nights, deserve to cry your eyes out and be listened to and held all night until you fall asleep safely in his arms.

What if I told you that you could have all of that and so much more?

It's true, you know. You just have to take that first step.

That first step. Sure, you've heard it a million times.

But think about it. If you don't take it today, then what about tomorrow? What if you don't take it tomorrow? What if you never take it? What if you wake up one day and put your hands to your face and trace the wrinkles of time, wondering where your life went, wondering why he's not lying next to you?

It's up to you. Some go their whole lives and never find it because they refuse to believe they deserve it.

But you do deserve it.

Whoever told you that you didn't deserve to fall in love? To feel loved?

Whoever hurt you in the past is gone. Where are they now? Who are they to tell you that you can't love someone?

Have you forgotten that they're only human too?

The only thing you need to listen to is the rhythm of your own beating heart.

Oh, it's still beating. Listen carefully. Can you hear it? Such a beautiful sound.

Their heart is beating too, you know. Beating for none other than you. Can't you hear it?

Your heart was meant to love. You are meant to be held by someone who loves and cares about you. You are meant to make love on cool spring nights between claps of thunder, meant to lie on blankets and look up at the stars together, meant to take walks through the park in autumn holding hands. Your lips are destined to kiss passionately and your body held tightly in the moonlight as he wraps his arms around you and whispers "You're my everything, I love you" into your ear.

You can make all the excuses in the world, but deep inside you know it's true.

So what are you waiting for?

Follow the sound of your own heartbeat. Listen to it speaking to your soul, longing to love again and to feel loved.

You're going to be happy. You're going to feel the purest joy and the most wonderful compassion you've ever experienced.

All it takes is one step, and five words: "I'm worth more than this."

Give it a shot.

I don't think you'll regret it.

Slide

When are you going to realize that when you find your prize you can't just hide inside?

What will it take for you to shake the feelings of yesterday so horrible they make you wake from nightmares that make your heart break?

Why do you ghost them when you know in your soul they carry with them a hymn you can truly believe in?

Does disappearing solve anything? Does it feel better to swing from fling to sting, chasing after that shiny, expensive diamond ring?

That diamond ring won't mean a thing if this mockingbird don't sing.

Why hide the feelings you feel trapped inside your heart that's so full of all those tears you've cried? Open up your heart wide and let those tear drops slide into the dark pit where all those terrible memories so long ago died.

The future is now, there's no turning back. It's time to pick yourself up and get on the right track. Love is still waiting for you and there's no time to slack.

Only you can choose to love again and I know you'll find true happiness my friend, because pure hearts always win in the end.

It's been proven time and again.

Swallow

I'd swallow you whole if I could, but your bitter taste is so bold it leaves my tongue feeling cold.

Each lie, each deceptive word, every morsel chokes like swallowing a sword.

How can such beautiful lips be so toxic? How can an angel's voice sound so neurotic, such a sharpened mind act so psychotic?

Taking pills was never my thing anyway. My medication days are done and you're the biggest one I've ever choked on.

No amount of water could rinse down this feeling of regret, that searing pain inside my chest you always cause me to get.

You're like acid, climbing right back up and spilling out of my mouth, forming a twisted concoction the size of lake placid.

You're bad for my health, poisonous to my soul. The shape that you're in could never fill the space in this empty hole.

You've been spoiled for far too long, been the subject of too many half-hearted love songs.

You're rotten to the core, ignoring the stench of your own disgusting soul as you cry and beg for more and more.

You hunger for a love that's gourmet, but you've wasted too much time looking for lovers like a zombie binging on a rancid buffet.

You're a tough act to swallow, and I'm already full from your bullshit.

So take your forks and knives elsewhere, find someone else's heart to poke, stab and slit.

Just make sure you keep my hunger out of it.

"No matter the depth, the message remains the same: whenever we are lost, sometimes it's better to go back from whence we came." — The Ghosts

An Ending

I remember placing my hand on your chest, feeling the thumping beat of your heart grow faster and faster.

"I'm so scared, honey," you whispered to me.

I told you everything was going to be ok.

But I knew it wasn't going to be.

I tried my hardest to fight the tears. Tried so hard to force a smile on my face.

But inside I wanted to break down, cry like a scared, helpless child.

But I remained strong, at least on the outside, for you.

Your heartbeat began to slow down.

"I love you."

Hearing you say those three words to me, even here at the end of the road, felt just as magical as it did the first time you spoke them to me.

"I love you too, sweetheart."

Never before had I meant those words more than I did on that day, in that very moment. They were the last words I ever spoke to you.

Your eyes slowly closed...and you smiled one last time.

And with one strong final heartbeat, the rhythm suddenly stopped.

"Goodbye," I whispered in your ear.

I couldn't hold it in any longer. I wrapped my arms tightly around you and wept like I've never wept before. I moaned and groaned, I apologized over and over, wished for you to come back, cursed at God for letting this happen to you, and I felt like a broken-down pile of emotion.

Damn, I loved you.

And I still do, you know.

It's been five years, and I don't know if you can hear me right now, but my heart still belongs to you.

I promised you that not even death would keep us apart, and I meant it.

I'm laying these flowers on your grave, not because you're gone, but because I want to remind you that as long as there are flowers to bloom, my love for you will do the same, season after season.

Your passing was so beautiful, so poetic. You went out of this world as gracefully as you had lived in it. I can only hope to do the same, but I doubt I'll be so lucky. I can't imagine a more beautiful sight than seeing you smile one last time.

I've been taking dance lessons, you know. Remember how I told you I'd save a special dance for you up in heaven? And do you remember how you used to tease me about it? "Well, Mr. two left feet, if you want to dance with me in the next life, you'd better learn how to dance in this life first!"

I promised you that I'd get around to it. But then life happened. Kids happened, parents passing away happened, and life seemed to get in the way.

Well, you'll be happy to know that I've kept my promise. We meet every Saturday at the high school gym.

And would you believe that these old bones still have some groove left to them?

Never knew I could cut a rug like that. You're probably laughing right now hearing me say that, but just wait till I get up there, honey. I'm going to blow your mind, sweep you off your feet and swing you to the moon!

You know, some people say they believe that when we get to Heaven, we're all young and beautiful. But you know what? If you looked just as beautiful as the day you passed away, I'd be perfectly content. Funny thing about love is, you don't see someone's physical appearance any more after a while. All you see is a radiant angel standing before you. And that's what you'll always be. My radiant angel.

Can you hear that, honey? Can you hear the crickets conducting their evening symphony? That's our song they're playing, honey. And soon, we'll dance to that beautiful song for all eternity.

And next time I look into your eyes and you smile at me, we'll never have to say goodbye again.

Fallen Angel

The instant she slit her second wrist, she immediately regretted her decision.

No one told her how painful it feels.

No one told her how deeply she had to cut.

As blood poured from her arms, her life began to flash before her.

"Oh God, what have I done?"

She began to panic, quickly trying to put her hands over the wounds, but it wasn't working.

It was like a bad dream. A nightmare she couldn't wake up from. In those last final moments of her life, time slowed down.

Was it worth it? Was teaching Joey a lesson worth taking her life over?

Was her heart really broken, or could she have mended it?

Suddenly 15 doesn't seem like a very long time to live. Suddenly the years ahead seem far more numerous than those behind her.

But it's too late.

"This is it. My God, this is...."

"....Why...?"

"Oh God, why?"

Suddenly her dad rushes into the bathroom.

"Honey? Oh god what did you do? What did you do?!"

"Dad?"

"Shh. I've got you, sweetheart."

"I'm...scared."

"It's ok, honey. It's going to be ok."

Susie looked up at her father with tearful eyes filled with regret, confusion, and terror.

"Dad, I'm...sorry..."

Susie's dad held her tightly as she spoke her last words, before losing consciousness and dying in his bloody arms.

Teardrops streamed endlessly down his face and onto the floor, mixing in with the pools of blood.

Susie's dad would remember this moment for the rest of his life. He would spend many sleepless nights awake, crying on the edge of his bed. He'd thought about joining her at times, thinking it would be easier if he'd just pull the trigger and meet her on the other side.

"What's the point of living when you've lost your angel?" he'd think to himself.

Life never was quite the same for Dan. He'd relive that moment in his nightmares for the rest of his life. Wondering where he went wrong, what he could have done to prevent this. He battled depression, hit the bottom of countless bottles, did some soul searching in a variety of different sanctuaries, but nothing seemed to help.

When Dan finally passed away at age 74 of cancer, he'd felt his entire life was a waste. Felt like he failed her all those years ago. He never got over it, never slept another peaceful night, never forgave himself.

When James and Jenny Yates purchased Dan's old house after he'd passed, they were shocked to find that Susie's bedroom door was shut. When Jenny turned the knob and opened the door, she found that Susie's room was exactly the way she'd left it over 30 years ago. On the nightstand next to her bed was an envelope. Jenny picked it up, put her hand gently on her pregnant belly, and opened it.

Inside was a hand-written note from Dan.

"If you find this note, I pray that you don't make the same mistakes I did. If you have a child, love them like there's no tomorrow.

Make every single day count."

"To those who love their children dear, I pray these words you read will be clear.
Don't make the mistakes I made, heed these words before time fades.
In the middle of the night, tuck them in so tight, never let them fade from sight.
Cherish every laugh, every tear. Remind them you love them year after year.
And when times get tough, don't ever give up. Whether a death in the family or a terrible break up.
Be there for them as they grow up. Regardless of what happens, hold them in your arms tightly before their time is up.

Listen to them when they speak, even while their fragile hearts are still so weak.

There is love and desperation in every word, regardless of what you think you've heard.

You are their protector, the light in their life, through every struggle, through every strife.

Teach them to make every moment last, that life is more than perfect photographs.

Show them that they are valuable, that life is always worth living and this world is magical.

And when they whisper "I love you" in your ear, listen carefully to those words and cherish them so dear.

Because one day you may wake up and no longer hear them. One day they may be gone, and you may never hear "I love you" again.

My story is over but a new one will soon begin. I hope you'll be inspired by the words I've written with this pen.

Because they're here today but gone tomorrow.

And it's up to you whether this story ends with a smile or with sorrow."

A tear streamed down Jenny's face. She looked down at her belly and rubbed it gently.

"Our story will have a happy ending, won't it?"

A cool summer breeze drifted by, embracing them with gentle reassurance. Outside the clear blue sky, the warm sun rays shined bright as two cloudy figures were reunited by the same reassuring breeze. An old story ended. A new one began.

Vale

I'm sorry I had to leave you. I'm sorry for the pain I've caused you.

We aren't guaranteed tomorrow, and I'm sorry I promised you we'd have that together.

I didn't know that when I kissed you on the cheek last night that it would be the last time. Didn't know it would be the last time I'd look into those beautiful eyes.

Didn't know when I started up my car that it would be the last time I'd adjust the rear view mirror so I could see you waving at me as I drove away.

Didn't think I'd leave you that night and never come back.

When you saw what was left of the car on the news that night, did your heart sink into your chest? Did you fall to the floor in tears?

The worst part about being on the other side is that you can't reach out and touch someone. Can't wrap your arms around them and whisper in their ear that you're ok, that they're going to be ok.

I'm sorry I left you.

I'd do anything to come back. Just to look into those eyes one more time.

I'm sorry it was my time to go. Sorry for all the broken promises I can't keep.

I'm sorry you're alone. Sorry you can't move on.

Does it hurt when you think of me now? Knowing that my flesh is rotting under six feet of soil? Knowing that if you saw my face right now, it would horrify you?

Remember me as I was that night.

Remember my smiling face as I said goodbye.

Savor that final kiss.

When you can't sleep at night, close your eyes and whisper my name. When your warm breath passes over your soft lips, you'll feel mine gently pressing against yours.

I'm sorry I left, but I promise you that one day you'll see me again.

That's one promise I know I can keep.

Fantasy

My love, my soul longs to connect with yours. With every passionate kiss, I draw nearer to you. With each gentle touch I can feel you, inside and out.

Let's get lost in these sheets. Under this dark canopy we'll be transported to a world of romance, a fantasy of ecstasy that's only ours to indulge in. Mountains will rise and warmth will flood through our bodies. We'll grab the stars, pull them down to us and sink into oceans of loving pleasure.

Our bodies will dance passionately in a symphony of indulgence as fireworks ignite around us.

When you hold me tightly you will know that I am all yours. My body belongs to you alone. I want to climb inside you and become one with you in body and spirit while we explode together in a supernova of euphoric love.

You will taste my love for you on my lips, feel it in the way I touch you, hear it in my passionate cries.

Every day you'll turn me on like the sun, every night you'll make me glow like the moon.

My passion for you will never die, and I'll always be ready to make this fantasy with you a reality.

Dear Son

I wish I could show you what it's like to wake up in the morning and walk down the stairs to the sound of mom and dad discussing work stories over breakfast.

I wish we could decorate a Christmas tree together as a family, lay outside and take turns counting the shooting stars.

I wish I could take you on a fun road trip where mom and dad sing silly songs together and tell corny jokes while you sit in the back seat rolling your eyes at us.

I wish you had a mother to tuck you in at night and kiss you goodnight after I kneel down beside your bed and pray with you.

I wish you could see your dad fall in love with someone and be a positive example to you of how a real man should treat a woman.

I wish I could find someone to give my heart to so that you'll know what it means to be selfless and share your love with another.

I wish your world hadn't been shattered at such a young age. There are many things in this life we can't control. And words can't explain how

sorry I am for that. You're too young for me to explain it to you now, but someday you'll understand I did everything I could to make it work.

I'm just thankful that we have each other. You and I, we are going places, buddy.

This whole world could crumble away, but as long as you're here with me, it would be just fine.

This journey was meant for you and I. Where it will lead us, I can't say. But there's no finer companion to take with me.

We are just two lost souls, trying to figure this life out together, aren't we?

So let's do this. Let's conquer this life together. And I'll protect you each and every day, love you like there's no tomorrow and carry you through the darkness ahead.

There are many bright days ahead, and one day we will find our place in the sun, together.

"Beautiful on the outside, wicked inside. Your rotten core became harder and harder to hide. When the blonde curls lose their bounce and your dignity is stripped ounce by ounce, what is left to find?" – The Ghosts

Forgotten

Find someone before you find yourself lost and all alone.

With each tick of the clock, another flame flickers out, another chance for happiness disappears.

Find them before you wake from your slumber, before you emerge from your comfortable coma.

Walk away from square one before you have to play their games, hold onto the dice before life rolls them for you.

Tell her you love her while you still have the chance, go to that party you know she'll be at, click "send" on that message you've tried writing her a thousand times before.

I never planned this, never asked for a broken heart falling apart inside my chest. I thought marriage was forever, thought love could right all wrongs, set me free, thought it would cement together those castle walls we were supposed to build in the clouds.

No one told me the future would be paved with cracked whores and choking weeds, the oceans filled with lost souls drowning in PTSD and valleys would be filled with uppers and downers wandering like zombies for their next fix.

I never imagined our minds would be plucked from our brains, lost in someone else's reality, never thought a bed could feel so cold and lonely.

We are the fuck-ups and the fucked up, the users and the used, the vampires and the crimson vessels.

We've had the life sucked out of us, we've given all, taken all, and received nothing but dishonesty, disloyalty, and dismay with poisonous doses of unfaithfulness, jealousy and hatred.

Recognize us.

Acknowledge us.

Remember us.

We never really went away. In this purgatory of broken dreams we still exist like ghosts, vapors of long forgotten days.

We were once your former lovers, those you dreamed about at night, those you poured your heart out to through the ink of pens, onto fancy colored parchment, in digital words feverishly typed with our blistered thumbs.

We are your former playthings, the teddy bears you'd snuggle with each night, the tin soldiers who used to stand up for you so valiantly.

Time is ticking away, the winds of change are blowing and you can't stop them. Nothing can stop the wheels from turning, the seasons from changing.

Find her before you miss her. Kiss her before you have to wave goodbye. Remember her before you're forgotten. Laugh with her before you cry. It's not too late, there's still time. Don't make the same mistake we did. Save yourself from the hell of goodbyes, dear john letters and farewell texts.

Time waits for no one, and neither does love.

Don't let yourself sink into the ocean waves waiting for your ship to come. Listen to the whispering of our voices, the ghosts who have been long forgotten.

Find her before what's left of you is gone.

Find her before you too become a ghost of this abandoned home.

Endless

I'm 14 years old. I step onto the school bus and I'm greeted with your beautiful smile and the most stunning eyes I've ever seen. I smile back at you, and we both look down and blush. I really want to sit down next to you but I'm too shy to say anything.

I'm pushing you in a wheelchair to the front door of the doctor's office. As we approach the door a young man holding his girlfriend's hand approaches us. "Let me get that for you two," the man says, and holds the door open for us.

We both glance at the couple and smile at them before looking into each other's eyes and smiling before I push you into the building.

We are driving down a country road after a beautiful spring day adventure. The windows are rolled down and "Say you will" comes on the radio. "That's our song, honey!" You shout excitedly. My excitement is in equal measure and my breath is taken away for a moment as I reach over and grab your hand and smile at you. "I love you so much," I tell you.

I'm driving you home after an exhausting day of treatment. I look over at you and you look so tired, but you're still the most beautiful woman I've ever laid eyes on. "Honey," I tell you, "I'm still the luckiest man in the universe."

Instantly your eyes light up as you smile at me. "No one is luckier than this girl," you tell me while a tear streams down your cheek.

The kids are in bed and we are finally left alone to enjoy our evening together. I'm putting a movie in for us to watch as you walk into the kitchen to make some popcorn. "What do you want to drink, honey?" You ask me.

And as I raise my eyes up from the tv and look into the kitchen, I see you standing there and I'm speechless, because I'm awestruck by your beauty. And for a moment I just stand there with a big smile on my face and can't find the words to say. You tilt your head like you always do and smile back at me. "I love you," you tell me softly.

My heart skips a beat as I reply with the same three words, those words I've spoken to you a thousand times that never lose their meaning. And it's moments like these where we feel so alive together. So in love.

I'm sitting on the couch talking to our daughter on the phone. "I'm so proud of you, honey," I tell her. She's just accepted a very prestigious job and tells me she's expecting her third child. "Tell mom I love her for me, ok?" She says. I assure

her that I will, and I smile as my eyes begin to water. I hang up the phone and walk into the bedroom, and you're lying on the bed asleep. I stand in the bedroom doorway for a moment, and smile. "There's the love of my life," I whisper. "Still as beautiful as ever."

I walk over to the machine that's helping you breathe and check to make sure everything is in order, but I can't concentrate because I keep looking at your beautiful white hair flowing onto the pillow. I slowly reach down and move my fingers through your soft hair. I smile just like I always do when I'm with you, and the corners of my eyes wrinkle up. "Gosh, what a beauty."

Then I give you a kiss on your forehead and tell you that I love you.

We are standing on a bridge overlooking a river. A subtle breeze blows through your hair as I turn to look at you. You smile at me as I brush your hair out of your face to kiss you.

"Our love is like this river," I tell you. "This river flows endlessly, and so too does our love. It will never, ever stop." You smile and nod your head in agreement and lean in to kiss me again.

I've been up all night with you in this small hospital room. The constant sound of beeping machines ring through my ears. It could be any moment now, and I don't want to miss the chance to say goodbye to you before you go. I hold your hand tightly and try to fight back the tears, but I can't. I start thinking of all the wonderful memories we've shared though, and I smile, wiping away the tears. "We've made a lifetime of happy memories, honey." I tell you. "Far too many good memories for me to be sad right now. And I know that's how you'd want it to be."

I smile, knowing that our love for each other isn't just confined to the years we've spent on earth. My heart is comforted knowing that we will be together even in the next life. And that we will be able to spend eternity together.

We are watching Our children play together in the park. We're sitting on a bench together holding their half-eaten snow cones; and our hands are sticky from them but we can't hold back the laughter as Our daughter is being chased by Our son with a little plastic green snake. We laugh so hard our faces start to hurt.

I'm lying in a bed, staring up at the ceiling. I can't move my body, but I can hear two voices in the room with me. "We're here, dad, one of them tells me. "Hi dad, I hope you're having a good day! Your grand-daughter wanted me to tell you hi, and she hopes you get better soon!" Another voice tells me. I can't see them, and I don't recognize their voices, but somehow I know that I love them, and they love me too. And that's enough.

I'm stepping onto the bus again, and when I reach the top step I turn and see you sitting there in a seat by yourself. "Is there room for one more?" I ask you. "Of course there is, honey. I've been saving this seat for you," you reply with that beautiful smile on your face. And then I sit down beside you, look into your beautiful eyes, and we smile at each other.

Rocket Ship

If I could build a rocket, and put all my thoughts, all my feelings, all my dreams into it, how far would it soar? How high would it fly into the sky? If I decided to break free from this bubble, from this tiny world I call home, what adventures would I find? What places would I go?

If I could take you along with me, would we find what we've truly been looking for? Would we reach for the stars and pull them down to us? Would we see sights yet unseen? Hear sounds our ears can not imagine? Would the ocean be big enough to hold our dreams? Would the mountains be tall enough to measure up to the heights we would climb? Take my hand, and let's find out. There's still time left. Still time to start that journey, still time to leave it all behind and start anew.

Wave goodbye to darkness, say hello to happiness. Here's a kiss to build a dream on as we're dancing cheek to cheek. Unforgettable adventures await, and there ain't no mountain high enough to stop us.

Faraway

I can't hope anymore because I can no longer feel. I can't crawl because I have no arms left to embrace, can't hear because I've shut them out. I can't sleep anymore because I can't wake up, can't breathe because I've run out of air.

I can't taste because I've held my tongue, can't scream because I've silenced my voice.

If this was war then I hope you're happy you've won. Does it satisfy you to know I'm waving the white flag, surrendering what's left of my heart to a battlefield scattered with remnants of what once were our hopes and dreams?

Was it worth it? Was this victory worth the deluge of tears, stretching your heart out paper thin, ripping my heart to shreds to feed your insatiable hunger for affection?

When war is over, who wins? When the casualties are counted, who lives?

Brokenness is certain. The aftermath was filled with hatred. Wounds cut deep.

And when it's all over, the only thing that's guaranteed is uncertainty.

"I went back in time to kill the old me, but found out it wasn't as satisfying as I thought it would be." — The Ghosts

The Ghost

They call me The Ghost.

If you burn me I'll vaporize before your eyes.

I'll whisper sweet nothings into your ear,

take your heart and soul on a journey far away from here.

I'll enter inside you and make you feel loved,

I'll take you so high and show you what the world looks like from up above.

To love me is to die like me. To make love to me is to drown your soul in a burning sea.

To be eternally mine is to let go of your senseless fears, and get lost with me as we burn like stars and shine.

I am The Ghost, a legend foretold. I'm as ancient as time itself, just as mysterious, almost as old.

I'll be the fear that creeps into your dreams, the passion that lights you up under the sheets, an orgasmic quake between the seams.

My thoughts will make your mind explode, bring you to your knees, erase your selfish ego and haunt your humble abode.

I'll be your pleasure if you'll let me in.

I'll be your pain if you'll succumb to your sin.

Don't fight a vapor you can't control. Choose to love me and I promise I'll give you my heart and soul.

It's time for me to go, my time here is now over.

Next time you find me, call my name if you're interested in crossing over.

Echoes

Somewhere out there, the past echoes with warm, soothing memories calling us back to what we've spent our whole lives running from.

All this time we've been moving forward, never taking the time to turn around and see the truth.

Can you hear the music? The sound of yesterday playing softly in your ears? Listen carefully. Let it take you home.

Swing sets rust in empty backyards, buried memories rot into the earth, forgotten by time. The wind howls over the field we once played red rover in. The screams and laughter of yesterday still echo subtly through the atmosphere. Can't you hear it? Though our young voices were silenced so long ago, our ghosts still burn in the air, our smiles still shine brightly through the darkness.

Take a picture in your mind, a moment of time when laughter was all we knew. Hold on to that moment, and never forget it.

Lonely

Thoughts come and go, but most die before they grow.

My mind is a hurricane of ideas that sometimes make me fall to my knees.

Where do these words come from? Do they drip from the lips of those below, or are they sung from the chords of angels above?

I'm building castles with no real purpose, while a flood of memories rises to the surface.

Perhaps it is a curse to see the world as I do. If only I could be as carefree as the rest of humanity, see it from their point of view.

How can I feel like the world desires me, yet feel as if no one truly wants my company?

To be on top is truly the loneliest of places. Whatever glory exists up there is washed away when you miss looking into their beautiful faces.

What sadness can be defined by a man whose only purpose is to find peace of mind?

I've been shaped by fire, I've been redefined. I've gained valuable wisdom, and left the past behind.

I've sought all the things that the wise ones told me to seek out. I've crossed every bridge, eliminated every doubt.

But still it's not enough, because I still don't have what my heart desires: to find companionship and love, to ignite together our heart's eternal fires.

But perhaps eternity comes for me without a flicker or spark, only the shell of a man who's left with an empty heart.

"Find me before what's left of me is gone, before these shadows close in on me. Save me before there's nothing left worth saving." — The Ghosts

Mindful

Fragments of photographs like puzzle pieces drift through the cerebellum. Thoughts flow through currents of adrenaline, retracing memories back to the amygdala.

I want this to stop. I want these memories to end, I want the past to be erased.

But it's no use. The pills I take, the chemicals I inhale, can't seem to take away the painful parts.

If I could take a knife and pry out my eye, maybe the bad dreams would ooze from the empty socket.

If I could send a snake up my nose, maybe it would slither its way to my brain and sink its sharp fangs into my cerebral cortex, spreading deadly poison across the landscape of my broken thoughts.

Maybe if I think hard enough, maybe if I try, my mind would explode and shatter into a thousand pieces, so no one would ever be able to put it back together again.

I don't want to think any more. I don't want to feel. I've had enough of everything for one short lifetime.

Is this depression embedded in my DNA? Do I suffer from the sorrows of my ancestors?

Are the chemicals in my brain imbalanced? Are these misfired neurotransmitters a lie?

Why did God make me this way? Why did God design us this way? Why can't we be perfect too?

I guess we don't deserve it. After all, we are wicked creatures who don't use our brains like we should.

I suppose if that's the case then what's the point in thinking anyway?

Scarecrow

I'm not half the man I thought I was.

Thought I'd lived and learned, tried to mature and grow - now I'm just a scarecrow.

I was on top of the world, thought I'd seen it all.

Now my lifeless body hangs in a lonely field, filled with straw.

I traveled down my yellow brick road, thought I'd find gold.

But only a deep, dark pit found me at the end of that road.

So I turned around and walked back to the start.

But by the time I got back, I'd fallen apart.

The crows came down and pecked at my stuffing.

No lungs left to breathe, but still I lay there huffing and puffing.

How could I breathe if I was made of straw? Maybe I wasn't so artificial after all.

Maybe I was more human than I realized. Maybe I wasn't the person I thought the world despised.

With every ounce of my strength I pulled myself back together, each piece of straw carefully tethered.

And for a second, I thought I felt the pumping of blood, felt my heart start beating and filling back up with love.

In the heat of the sun and the buzzing of flies, slowly I sat up, and began to rise.

But when I stood up, no one was around. No one to guide me, no hope to be found.

So I pondered, "Why do I exist?". What is my true purpose amid all of this?

I thought for a moment but came up with nothing, and slowly my organs and tissue turned back into stuffing.

As I looked around, I was all alone. All I could think of was how far I'd have to roam.

Out of the corner of my eye, a wooden post poked out of a cornfield. And when I saw it, I knew my fate had been sealed.

As I limped towards the corn, with my last breath I mourned.

I knew my destiny all too well. I was destined to rot in this green and yellow hell.

So I climbed onto the post, stretched my arms out wide. If my eyes still had tears, I most certainly would have cried.

For a moment life seemed beautiful, for a moment I seemed alive. But I guess it's better to have lived for a moment, than having never tried.

Long ago I longed to grow. Now I hang from this rotting post, hopeless as a scarecrow.

Love's Requiem

If love is your god, consider me an atheist.

I've subscribed to your religion of passion.

I've drank holy water from your lips, indulged in holy communion with your body, yet still I thirst.

I've partaken in the sensual bread of your flesh, and it's left me with ravenous hunger.

I've been baptized in the river of your promises, been lost in your sacrament of divine pleasure.

I've entered into your temple and sacrificed my heart at your altar.

But the darkness in your soul started seeping through the cracks in your angelic visage.

I've grown wise to your false prophecies, your blasphemous temptations.

You tried to pull me back as I backslid into hypocrisy. But I broke free from your commune, escaped your cult of selfish desires.

Now love is dead to me.

Crumbled like a sacred statue, in pieces on the ground.

My heart has hardened, I've accepted my fate.

Better for my heart to burn eternally than to spend another night in your bed of lies.

Lover

Some look to the heavens for love, some search endlessly for it. When I think of true love found, I look across the room and see her standing there, holding that glass of red wine.

The perfect vision of beauty, her Italian hair illuminated in the sun's rays as she gazes out the window into the city streets below.

That's my angel.

Passionate kisses taste like wine, my lips against her skin on every inch of her heavenly body, gasping for breath as we get lost in an ocean of passion.

To touch the love of one's life is to enter into the gates of paradise, to feel heaven's warmth and taste euphoria in its purest form.

When she gazes into my soul with those beautiful ocean eyes, I want to get lost in her galaxy, swim in her Milky Way, fall into a sea of stars and let gravity pull me inside her.

One more glass of wine. Let's dance in the kitchen with our clothes off, sway to the harmony of our infinite love, get lost in each other as time stands still and the world becomes ours.

She is everything, and my heart beats for her eternally.

Every touch, every glance, every deep breath, every sigh, every cry brings us closer to eternity.

In this seventh-floor apartment we found truth, passion, trust, ecstasy, and love.

I want to forever share these red wine kisses, make her my misses, and celebrate everything that this incredible bliss is.

This is us. We are love.

This is love. Eternally.

Some people speak volumes with thundering
vocals, others make their message loud
and clear through protests, swinging
their powerful messages through the air.
Calamus Gladio Fortior - The Ghosts

The Clockwork Knight

The clockwork knight, wound up so tight, searches for his princess all through the night.

Make haste, make haste, for another's lips she'll soon taste.

The gears inside his mechanical heart turn and grind, reminding him of what he left behind.

This endless chasing is such a hassle, for his princess, she's in another castle.

As the seconds march by, he wonders if he'll find her before he dies.

Tick tock, Tick tock, his search will soon come to an abrupt stop.

For there In the sanctuary as he peers through the stained glass, he catches a glimpse of her as she shouts, "You've come at last!"

But before he could move, the Knight's heart began to shake.

Tick, tock, tick...

Too late, his heart did break.

Nightfall came and the poor knight stood motionless, helpless but brave, as he watched her being taken away.

The Clockwork Knight's quest ended that night, severed by faulty mechanics that created his plight.

Stories you see, they often have happy endings. But this one? Well, that happy ending is still pending.

Tick, tock, tick, tock...

Luna

The stars reflect so beautifully in your eyes tonight, luminous reminders echoing into my soul from your passionate gaze.

Let's count the stars together, shall we? For as long as we can count our lives will go on, never burning out until the last star fades slowly from existence.

Look at the moon, my dear. Let's gaze into its white mystery. Let's ponder the mysteries of life as we dive deep into its craters.

Tonight the moon exposes its heavenly body for all the world to see. It isn't hiding behind the cover of darkness, as if it wants to shine its spotlight upon us as we embrace in the night air.

What good is a moon's glow without the stars to compliment it? Like an orchestra, they play their ethereal symphony, playing our favorite song while the crickets chirp in perfect harmony.

Tonight our love will be projected into the night sky, penetrating the atmosphere, soaring across the universe to be seen by two extra-terrestrial lovers standing on some distant shore.

Tonight our passion will float upward into the darkness like a glowing tapestry, wrapping itself around the stars, collecting them for us to hold in the palms of our hands.

I never want to let go.

You never want to let go.

Let's never let go.

And may this moon's gravity forever hold us together.

Expand

It's time to hold nothing back. I'm tired of running this race of rats.

Thought I'd disappeared now it's time for a comeback.

I'm scratching off these scars that remind me of those days when the world was ours.

This heart is mine, and belongs to no one.

I've fought hard, I've run the race. Battles lost, battles won.

When all you have left is yourself, there's no one left to conquer, no time left to falter.

In my mind's eye I can see it so clear. A beautiful future somewhere far away from here.

A place devoid of you, a vast ocean filled with infinite shades of blue.

These wings are sprouting and I think it's time for me to fly.

Time to soar, never look behind me and leave you here to die.

I am all that matters. The world is mine, and I'll take it and leave this hell while everything around you shatters.

I'm not sorry.

I have no remorse.

My hatred for you will fuel me.

I'm on the right course.

Swing

She's a ghost, a vapor burning in the playground's bubble, trapped amongst the smiling faces, the optimistic glow that each one of them carries.

They all come from realms of stability, planes of a prosperous existence, while she swings up and down into highs and lows, crawling slowly through life as if she were still an infant.

Laughter echoes off the walls of this recreational dome, becoming a piercing shriek that enters the canals of her ears, reminding her of something she'll never experience.

Behind her mask the tears flow freely. If only they could see. If only they could touch her face and feel the sorrows encapsulated in each and every tear.

Up and down she goes, wishing the chains would break off and she'd fly upward, away from here forever, to a place where she could finally remove her mask, breathe in the fresh air of hope, and dance in fields of jasmine under the warm rays of a comforting sun.

If only she could dream. If only such desires weren't ripped from her by the poltergeists inside her haunted home.

One day the world will know the beauty she keeps inside. One day the world will know her name, will see her precious face, and they will finally speak her name.

Valley

Her lips quiver as her heart shivers.

She lights up a cigarette, inhales the bitter taste of regret.

Her lungs hurt from weeping all night, knowing nothing she can do could ever make things right.

Counting the raindrops falling, a part of her still listens for him to start calling.

Tears hit the porch foundation in sync with the rain as her mind floats down a river of lost imagination.

Tonight memories will be her only friend, just pictures of what used to be that will never materialize again.

The seasons are cruel, of that there's no doubt. Where does she fit into life's tapestry? If she could write a book about her life, what would it be about?

She may never know.

And when the cold rain turns to snow, there's no telling where her mind will go.

"All I can do is hide this child inside me, hide my insecurities, hide my fears, cover up the confusion and hold back the tears." – The Ghosts

Town

This town's given all it can. Ashes are all that remain of the hearts once set ablaze by passionate dreams. Anger and apathy hang in the air like dense fog, suffocating the life out of the mindless wanderers that scrape the sidewalks with their heels.

It hurts to take a breath.

There is no hope here. No future filled with bright lights or the roaring of engines, no light at the end of this tunnel - nothing more than tear-soaked pavement and weeds choking the remnants of a once thriving community. The remnants of this desolate hole stay silent, but if you listen carefully you can still hear their cries carried through the howling wind.

If you close your eyes you can feel their dreams drifting past you, ideas tapping on your shoulder, grand visions of what once could be, but was never going to be.

This is where I call home.

When you come here, you lay down all your hopes and dreams and trade them for loneliness.

Joy traded for fear, hope traded for apathy, dreams traded for perpetual nightmares.

If I could kill myself maybe I could escape.

But I'm already a ghost.

It's already too late.

So I'll keep on living as if I am dying.

Dance

I've been saving this dance for my final

Romance. I've been saving this song for the one I've been waiting on

for so long.

You're my angel up in heaven, my one in a million, lucky number seven.

Come on down from the clouds if God will allow.

Strike up the band, I'll be ready when you land.

And I won't rest until we at last unite, hand in hand, sight to sight.

I knew you were out there, so I waited patiently, a thousand and two

years, basically.

All this time I've been composing this tune while waiting for our love

to bloom.

Many nights I'd stay awake, hoping for my fate to change.

But in the night air I could faintly hear a steady beat of two hearts, one

day destined to meet.

My heart beats stronger for you each day. Let this melody show you

the way.

Together

The stronger the love, the deeper the hate.

The shorter the string, the longer the suffering.

The weaker the heart, the stronger the comeback.

The more passionate the love making, the more the selfishness.

The more surreal the dream, the more depressing the reality.

The bigger the promises, the deeper the lies.

The sweeter the honey, the more rotten the waste.

The bigger the American Dream, the lonelier the two-bed-room apartment.

The bigger the church, the more hatred toward religion.

The bigger the heart, the smaller the compassion.

The more abundant the happiness, the deeper the depression.

Love is a race we run, where hatred isn't far behind.

And if hatred looms so near, do we truly ever love each other at all?

"How can your heart go numb after being so full of life for so long?" – The Ghosts

Scattered

I once was a man, whose thoughts and feelings spilled out onto the page in long lost nights of loneliness.

So many memories, once meaningful but now scattered into the winds of yesterday.

My head hovers above the clouds while my body's being dragged further into hell with each passing day.

The scent of depression lingers heavily in this desolate town. It soaks into our cracked skin, permeating throughout our broken bodies, killing us slowly but surely.

Unfocused thoughts, scattered shards of anger, hatred for lost souls, futile endeavors torn to shreds - everyday occurrences.

This world is collapsing. Can you feel it? Can you hear the fabric of reality being ripped right in front of us?

Listen closely and you'll hear the moans of these dark clouds echoing inside your soul. The sound is deafening.

Every day I sit and wait for the exit door to appear, but it never comes. Is this purgatory, or is it hell?

We search and pray for answers, but they never come.

So we'll wither away together, slowly disintegrating into nothing.

And after nothing, then what?

Magic

I wonder, does magic really exist?

Ask the pastors, the shamans and the scientists.

For if it hasn't yet been discovered, is it somewhere still waiting to be uncovered?

Is it hidden inside dusty ancient tomes, or kept secret in basements of abandoned homes?

Some say it's real, others say it's not. Whatever the case, for countless years it's been sought.

But I think those who say it's no longer here are quite wrong, and they've been wrong all along.

There's surely magic between you and I.

Because why else do I feel when I'm with you that I can fly?

Ponder

At what point will we stop believing we are invincible and start realizing that we are only human?

When will our heads finally be filled with the knowledge we seek? When will time finally stop so we can slow down and take everything in?

What will it take to heal the wounds we've given this world?

When will our hearts conquer our vanity? When will feelings give way to truth?

When will we start giving back to the earth what it's given us?

When will we realize that we don't have to wait for death to come in order to truly live?

Wind

When autumn comes knocking on your door, look for me where the leaves fall - that's where I'll be, scattered along the ground far away from the trees.

I'll let the wind carry me to destinations unknown. Don't worry about where I'll go. It doesn't matter where I end up, as long as it's somewhere far, far away from here.

Like a tree full of life in Spring I once felt the warm rays of the sun hit me, bringing me happiness as I danced to the sways of the breeze.

I held onto that happiness for as long as I could, even when the hot, dry months of summer took their toll on me.

But when that paranormal wind begins to blow, I'll find my way to lands unknown.

"The last time I saw your face, I erased the dreams we chased. It took a mere minute to fall from grace." – The Ghosts

Split

How long will we dance before we finally murder this romance?

We smile as we look into each other's eyes, but the truth is this house was built on lies.

Our hands connect and we feel that rush, but inside our hearts are being crushed.

Our bodies connect, but our souls are wrecked.

They claw at one another, scraping and stabbing, ripping apart and jabbing.

They scream and curse at one another, choking out what little life is left in them, until they're smothered.

As our lips meet this spiritual war comes to its peak.

If souls had blood we'd be drowning in it. If they had flesh we could hear it starting to split.

Deep inside we both know the truth: you'll kill me and I'll kill you.

And when it's all over, as zombies we will wander like we've got a bad hangover - until we find another life to destroy, rip their hearts out of their chest and snuff out what's left of their joy.

Yonder

Fleeting memories from the past, echoes that we thought would last.

Hearts broken, lives changed, in our mind's eye it's all the same.

I'm standing next to you on a sandy shore, the past tickling our feet once more.

So many years have passed us by, so many tears that we've wiped dry.

The past is gone, the future is ours.

Day by day, night by night, let's savor each moment and every hour.

Time will stop for no one but us. Let's build a foundation cemented by trust.

Shifting

Reality is shifting, the tapestry being rearranged, and history rewritten. The veil is being ripped apart.

Here we are at the end of the world, watching the cosmos drift into a new existence.

We're changing. Everything we know is changing.

Tomorrow we won't be the same. When we wake up, everything we once knew will be gone, as if it never happened.

Stars that once burned so brightly fall through the atmosphere like stones, replaced by sparks of new ideas, thoughts never imagined, and dreams never dreamt.

I should be scared. I should be terrified.

But here, at the end of the world, I am at peace.

Perhaps that's the scariest thing of all.

What happens when we cease to feel, when emotion is dead and fear becomes a distant memory?

If these wildfires are meant to forge us into better humans, if the striking of these hammers is sharpening our minds, maybe it's all going to be worth it in the end.

Perhaps the end of the world is the perfect place to be after all.

"There is surely magic between you and I;
Because why else do I feel that when I'm
with you, I can fly?" – The Ghosts

Sunlight

The sun peered through the windows of the small chapel, warming my back as I sat on the pew, reflecting on days gone by. A thousand different times I've sat here, thinking about what could have been, what should have been, and what really matters most in life. But in my searching my thoughts wandered off into futile dreams, losing sight of your holy presence. Distractions left and right tugged on me, and with fear and delight I embraced them. But with my wandering soul trying to escape, you pulled me back and told me that my place was here all along. Suddenly that which made no sense once again had meaning again. And in the warmth of the sunlight rays I felt your love shining down, reminding me that you're all that matters.

Reset

Brand new start, broken heart.

Wings off the ground, spinning round and round.

Like a roller coaster up and down, up and down.

Chest pounding hard, head about to explode. Can't stop thinking of those messages you wrote.

Rewind time, what good does it do? History repeats, I'm just another fool.

Silence speaks louder than words, the worst thing I've ever heard.

Anger sets in, tired of trying over and over again.

I'll take my heart back and carry on somehow, no energy or time to look back now.

Wasn't ready yet, but it's time to ride off into the sunset.

If I die then so be it, at least I tried.

At least I'll never have to worry about another goodbye.

Skin

I got tired of the skin I was in, so I ripped it to shreds as if it were paper thin.

Tired of them judging my exterior, sick of them seeing me as inferior.

One look in the mirror and my hideous visage became clearer.

I wasn't the man I thought I was on the inside. I could see it so clearly now that my skin was opened wide.

The decaying meat behind my shell reminded me of something that had crawled from the bowels of hell.

Panic set in as I fell to the floor, my hands soaked with crimson gore.

And as the blood poured from every orifice, All I could think was, "Is it too late to fix this?"

Spark

I know you've found a love you don't regret, but so long ago you could have picked me instead.

When your head hits the soft pillow, do you ever dream of the places we would go?

When you're left alone with your thoughts as your only friend the days seem longer as you wait for the end.

Falling leaves remind me of the days we spent working at the old mill, stealing glances at one another like thieves.

We were young and innocent then, untainted by the wages of war and sin.

I tried to hide behind the mask of a wise man, hoping you wouldn't notice what I had planned.

It was that look in your eyes that saw through my clever disguise.

One glance and I was hooked, ready again to spark up a new romance.

I played it cool, trying not to seem like a fool, but you caught me dreaming of what we could be.

By some miracle, seemingly out of the blue, as it turned out you felt the same way too.

"There aren't enough stars in the sky, not enough crashing waves to listen to, not enough letters to write, not enough shapes in the clouds to measure up to the heights your love brings me to." – The Ghosts

Sometimes

Sometimes I get tired of being human.

Sometimes I wish I didn't have to cry, didn't have to care, didn't have to love, didn't have to hate.

Some days I wonder if the world would be better off if I was nothing more than an object that couldn't feel.

Maybe then I wouldn't hurt anyone, wouldn't lie to them, wouldn't take from them, wouldn't need anything from them.

Sometimes I wish I couldn't see. Maybe then I wouldn't have to close my eyes when I go to sleep, wouldn't have to wipe my own tears, wouldn't have to witness the acts of violence, racism, discrimination and hatred of mankind.

Sometimes it gets tiring being human.

Sometimes I wish I didn't have to be.

Because maybe then the problem wouldn't be me.

Breathe

Today I looked at your picture and it took my breath away.

How do you do this to me?

It's hard enough to take a breath these days with the air as heavy as it's been.

I'd give my last breath if only to show you how much I love you, how much you mean to me, to show you that you're the greatest treasure ever worth finding.

When love is eternal, who needs to breathe? Everything I've ever wanted or needed is right here staring back at me with that beautiful smile and those ocean eyes.

If this world should pass away, and crumble into countless pieces or be destroyed in a cataclysmic event, our love would continue.

Who needs air when I'm breathing your love in each day? Who needs solid ground when I'm floating on cloud nine?

My heart is flesh but soul eternal. It is in the innermost depths of my soul, where my true heart resides that a place for you will always be, a place we call home together.

And even if the world ended today, there's no place like home.

Conundrum

Everyone wants to believe they're the hero of their own story.

I suppose in some ways we are all narcissists to varying degrees. At the end of the day we all want to be the center of our own universe, don't we?

But what happens if we wake up one day and realize that we aren't the hero of the story, but the villain?

Would we go on living, fooling ourselves into believing that what we were doing was the right thing, marching onward to the beat of our own drum, refusing to believe that we are a cancer to the reality we live in?

What if we came to the conclusion that the only way for our story to have a happy ending is to take the life of its main villain? Would we then take our own lives, knowing in our death the other characters in our story might thrive?

Knowledge is knowing that a tomato is a fruit. Wisdom is knowing not to put it in a fruit salad.

What if instead of admitting we are villains, we rewrote our stories entirely?

All of us are storytellers, really. Some tell stories with written word, others live out their stories through everyday routines. Some of us are great orators, using our voices to captivate, others are struggling through their own personal tragedies.

What will the story of your life look like when you're gone?

Will you be a hero or a villain?

I prefer to be a hero, even if I'm only fooling myself into believing so.

"Even villains find redemption sometimes, don't they? I wonder how many flakes of snow will pass me by as I ponder the reasons why I could never quite fly." - The Ghosts

Dedication

I would like to dedicate this book to my son Gabriel, who is a light in this sometimes dark world. I would also like to dedicate this book to all my loyal readers. Thank you for always believing in the Ghosts.

Thank you for reading these stories.
Look for more from The Ghosts in the future.

Until then stay ghostly and
keep haunting, my friends.